How Reference Works

SUNY Series, Scientific Studies
in Natural and Artificial Intelligence

Eric Dietrich, Editor

How Reference Works

Explanatory Models for Indexicals, Descriptions, and Opacity

Lawrence D. Roberts

State University of New York Press

Published by
State University of New York Press, Albany

© 1993 State University of New York

For information, address State University of New York
Press, State University Plaza, Albany, N.Y., 12246

Production by Diane Ganeles
Marketing by Fran Keneston

Library of Congress Cataloging-in-Publication Data

Roberts, Lawrence D., 1937–
    How reference works : explanatory models for indexicals,
descriptions, and opacity / Lawrence D. Roberts.
        p.   cm. — (SUNY series, scientific studies in natural and
artificial intelligence)
    Includes bibliographical references and index.
    ISBN 0-7914-1575-9. — ISBN 0-7914-1576-7 (pbk.)
    1. Reference (Linguistics) 2. Linguistic models. 3. Language and
logic. I. Title. II. Series.
P325.5.R44R63   1993
415—dc20   92-31942
                                                                 CIP

10 9 8 7 6 5 4 3 2 1

In memory of my parents,
Leo Joseph Roberts
and Marjorie E. Palmer Roberts

Contents

Acknowledgments

I am grateful to Binghamton University for support of my research for this book by granting not only a sabbatical leave but also a Dean's research semester. I also would like to thank Linacre College of Oxford University for accepting me as a senior member, and providing an ideal setting for my sabbatical work during an early draft of several chapters.

I am grateful to many people whose comments, criticisms, and encouragement have helped my work on reference. Among them are Jay Atlas, Gordon Baker, John Boler, Bruce Freed, Rom Harré, Albrecht Imhoff, Jack Kaminsky, John Lyons, John Moulton, Raymond Nelson, Mark Richard, Peter Strawson, John Sowa, Robert Weingard, and Howard Wettstein. I am especially thankful to my friends and colleagues, Jerry Aronson and Eileen Way, for many years of help and encouragement. Finally, I would like to thank the series editor, Eric Dietrich, for his support.

For bearing with me during my fixation on this book, I would also like to thank my wife, Pat, and my sons Max and Paul.

Chapter 2 is based on my paper "The Figure-Ground Model for the Explanation of the Determination of Indexical Reference," *Synthese*, 68 (1986) 441–486.

Lawrence D. Roberts
Program in Philosophy, Computers, and System Science
SUNY Binghamton

Abbreviations

"RE" for "referring expression" throughout the book
"DC" for "demonstrative and complement" in chapter 4
"IP" for "indefinite pronoun and individuating predicate" in
    chapter 4
"SUB" for "the principle of substitutivity" in chapter 7
"EG" for "existential generalization" in chapter 7

Chapter 1

An Introduction to Methodology:
Explanation, Specification, and Two Paradigms for
Theorizing about Language

Language is a much explored but largely unknown territory. Expeditions into it are guided by overall visions of it. The Chomskian perspective takes the key to language to be its *infinite productivity*: the capacity to produce an infinite number of grammatical sentences from a finite basis. In current analytical philosophy, most scholars focus on the *compositional nature* of sentences, which allows the meanings of sentences to be a function of the meanings of their parts. Productivity and compositionality I find interesting, but a different feature of language amazes me: that noises can convey meaningful content. For instance, I use noises to enable a person to understand my claim that a certain tree is likely to fall within the next few weeks. Or I use noises to request someone to hand me a particular red book that I am pointing at. How can our noises convey such content? This question targets the relational nature of language: how do these noises of language produce relations to things in the world and to other people?

The question of how meaningful content is present in language is wholly different from that of productivity, in that the latter is an intrinsic property of a system, whereas meaningful content is a relational property between symbols in a system and things outside that system. Questions about meaningful content are broader than questions about compositionality. The latter is one feature of meaning, concerning part-whole relations in meaning; this relation does not directly bring in the connection of meanings to speakers and the world, as does the question of how words have meaningful content. I don't intend to rank these questions in importance, because they are heuristic questions, which cannot be ranked until the results of the explorations are in. Rather, I want to point out that my question is different. It is also a traditional question, with traditional problems.

One problem with the question of how noises can convey content is that it raises issues about two relations at once, a relation to things in the world and a relation to people who understand the noises. Interestingly enough, the two traditional answers to the question are each based on a different one of these relations. One such answer is that meaningful content derives from the referential connection of words with things extrinsic to mind and language. Plato,[1] for instance, viewed meanings as based on the reference of words to eternal unchanging exemplars (the Platonic Forms) after which the material world is patterned. Later philosophers suggested that words might instead derive their meanings from referring to various other entities; among these were abstractions like universals or sets, or ordinary things in the material world. These theories get lumped together as *referential theories of meaning* because they all view meaningful content as arising from a referential relation between words and things. Gilbert Ryle (1957) caricatured such theories as the "'Fido'-Fido" theory: the meaning of the term 'Fido' is the dog Fido.

In contrast to referential theories, *ideational theories* view meaningful content in language as the result of a relation between words and ideas. On this view, a word gets its content from the ideas with which it is associated. Thus, ideas are taken to be intermediary devices linking words and things. *The Essay Concerning Human Understanding* by John Locke is probably the classical location for this theory, but versions of it circulated in medieval times and in the twentieth century, for example, in *The Meaning of Meaning* by C.K. Ogden and I.A. Richards. Also in the twentieth century, behaviorists developed a third theory of meaning. On this view, meaning is explained as a stimulus-response connection between the noises of language and behaviors: the noises are taken to be either stimuli for behavior, or responses to behavior.

All three theories of meaning encountered overwhelming objections (cf. Brown (1958) and Alston (1964)). I won't recount these, but will mention an interesting common feature in the trio. Underlying each theory is a fact about language, which was inflated into the essence of all language. For the *referential theory*, the fact is that words refer to things. For the *ideational theory*, it is that words are connected to ideas, and for the *behavioral theory*, it is that words are connected to behavior. These three facts cannot be ignored by any theory of how meaningful content connects with noises, but none of them provides the basic essence of language. Instead they contain phenomena of language that must themselves be explained.

The question of how meaningful content is connected with language has been in disfavor for years, and has been replaced to a large extent by questions about language that are mostly specificatory (the nature of these will be discussed shortly). Although I still find the question about the nexus of meanings and language interesting, I think that the general form of this question that I have been discussing is too broad to answer. Meaning in language has many levels. Because of this, there cannot be a single uniform theory of meaning in general, at least at the beginnings of theories of meaning. I distinguish the following levels of meaning in language: (a) lexical meaning for individual words, (b) reference made by means of noun phrases and other referring expressions, (c) the meanings of sentences (these include two different kinds of meaning: propositional content and speech-act meaning such as asserting or questioning), (d) Gricean implicatures (meanings that are implied but not logically entailed), and (e) meanings in figures of speech.

The best way to begin a study of how meaningful content connects with language is, in my opinion, to pick one of these levels of meaning, and develop an explanatory theory for it. This is what I propose to do. I will study reference made by means of *referring expressions*.[2] Such reference lies between lexical meaning and sentence meaning, in that it presupposes and uses the former, and makes a contribution to the latter. For example:

1. That horse is fast.

To figure out what (1) means as used in a context, one must figure out the referent of 'That horse,' which in turn requires that one use the lexical meanings of 'that' and 'horse' plus other factors like gestures and the context to determine the reference of 'that horse.' For brevity, I will often speak of the reference of referring expressions, even though my models are for the entire process involved in using referring expressions; this process includes speaker, hearer, words, actions, and context.[3] Once the reference of 'That horse' is discerned, it is contributed in some way to the meaning of the sentence as a whole.

My exploration of reference concentrates on indexicals (terms like 'this,' 'I,' or 'now') and definite and indefinite descriptions. I leave aside proper names because I view their mechanisms as relatively hidden, and best understood by comparison and contrast to other types of reference. Nor do I attempt to explain mechanisms underlying lexical meaning.

I picked the issue of the reference of referring expressions ('REs' for short) as a beginning to the study of the relation of words to things and thought, because REs link conversers with things in the world. In addition, reference is a central issue in twentieth-century philosophy, with well-defined problems and ample data. Some of these philosophical problems have been around since Gottlob Frege, the founder of the analytical tradition. For instance, how can we refer to the nonexistent, how are identity statements informative, or why is substitution of coreferential REs invalid in contexts of propositional attitude (contexts within the scope of verbs like 'believe that' or 'hope that')? There are still no generally accepted answers to these questions. Bearing on these problems about reference are data from communication, linguistics, and logical intuitions. Despite the importance of the problems and the availability of data, questions about reference to things in the outside world are relatively neglected in the Chomskian and compositional-semantic traditions. These schools do study reference, but concentrate on systems for representing reference and coreferentiality, rather than on how reference works in connecting words with things.

To answer the question of how reference works in connecting words and things, one needs an explanation. The view of explanation that I use is that of Rom Harré (1961), Jerrold L. Aronson (1984), and Fred I. Dretske (1981).[4] The goal, as Dretske (1981: 47) puts it, is "a more or less complete, precise, and systematic description of those entities and processes underlying the phenomena of interest." I devise models to clarify the underlying entities and processes which constitute reference. By a model, I do not mean a formal model, which is a set of objects that satisfy the axioms of a formal system. This type of model need not be explanatory, since it may use abstract data sets, rather than entities that resemble those underlying the phenomenon. Instead I have in mind a model that redescribes the phenomenon to be explained in terms of a set of entities which are simplified and abstract in comparison to real world entities, but still closely resemble the latter. For example, entities used in my models include the speaker, the hearer, the use of an RE, space-time locations, gestures, and descriptive content; also, relations of these entities are included in the models. These entities and relations closely resemble but are not identical to real world entities described by the same terms. This non-identity is needed because the real world entities and relations are more complex than those in my models. But we need the simplicity of the models to begin to find explanations. I view my models for reference as first steps, undoubtedly in need of further refinement.[5] Nevertheless, the differences between the models and the real world are small enough that the models provide explanations that tie diverse phenomena together in a clear way, and lead to further explanations and predictions.

Explanatory models differ from what I will call 'specificatory theories.' Because this distinction is unclear in current theories of language, and crucial to my approach to reference, I will discuss it at length. Specificatory theories prevail, in my opinion, in current theorizing about language, though philosophers and linguists often speak of them as explanatory.[6] Specificatory theories aim at providing clear and systematic specifications of all the phenomena in an area of study. Such theories may be bases for precise predictions, but, because they need not use conditions underlying the phenomena, they need not provide explanations. In place of underlying conditions, specificatory theories may use stipulations, circular devices, ad hoc devices, parallel entities, or results of the phenomena. Ptolemaic astronomy, for example, was a successful specificatory theory, which was refined over centuries to provide moderately accurate specifications for movements of heavenly bodies. These specifications had important applications in agriculture and navigation. Specificatory and explanatory devices may be mixed together in a theory, and a fully mature science has explanatory theories which also provide precise specifications.

Examples from the history of science will help to clarify the distinction between specificatory and explanatory theories. For instance, Johannes Kepler's descriptions of the solar system were very accurate at specifying motions, but the underlying mechanism he offered (the *anima motrix* of the sun) was inadequate. Thus, Kepler provided good specifications but weak explanations. Isaac Newton's laws, which included universal gravitation, provided the needed explanatory mechanisms.

Another example is the classification of the elements by their spectographic lines.[7] Each chemical element was known to have its own distinct spectographic pattern for some time before the discovery of the conditions and mechanisms underlying this phenomenon. Thus, a specificatory theory associated spectographic data with each element, even though this association was unexplained.

Niels Bohr's model of the atom provided a key ingredient in the explanation; electron rings plus mechanisms for energy absorption and radiation explained the spectographic differences.

A specificatory theory need not provide an explanation even if it is descriptively complete, that is, for every interesting property and relation in the real world, there is a corresponding value of a variable in the specificatory theory, and there are laws describing how the values of the variables are related. Kepler's laws of motion and the classification of the elements by spectographic lines approximated descriptive completeness without being explanatory. This does not mean that these specificatory theories were unimportant. Indeed, they were outstanding scientific achievements. My point is that when we have specificatory theories, we still hunger for more: we want to know the conditions and mechanisms underlying the specifications.

The history of science shows interactions of specificatory and explanatory theories. In the examples given above, specificatory theories existed without accounts of underlying conditions. In other cases, a partial theory about underlying conditions exists with little specificatory detail (e.g., early heliocentric theories of Aristarchus, Philolaus, and Hicetas,[8] or the early theory of genes as carriers of heredity). Each type of theory can stimulate the development of the other.[9] But science requires both aspects in its theories, so that it is a mistake to rest content in either type by itself. Moreover, when explanatory mechanisms are found for specificatory theories, they often provide more precise specifications of the phenomena. For instance, Newtonian specifications of planetary orbits included the gravitational effects of planets on each other. And explanations of one set of phenomena often are useful for explaining additional phenomena, for example, Bohr's model of the atom and its electron rings was used not only in explaining the spectra of elements but also in explaining chemical bonding.

In recent work in philosophy of language, specificatory theories predominate.[10] These theories aim at laying out in a systematic way (by rules or axioms) the truth conditions for all sentences of a particular language (or of a fragment of a particular language). The extent to which these theories are also explanatory for sentence meaning is unclear, and I will not discuss it here. Behind these theories lies an approach to theorizing about natural language which I call the *"predicate logic paradigm."*[11] Its current form has three features which affect the study of reference: it emphasizes (*a*) *translation into predicate logic*, and (*b*) *composi-*

tionality of meaning for sentences, and (*c*) it *separates semantics from pragmatics*. Each of these, I will argue, raises obstacles to developing explanatory theories of reference. Note that my focus is on the effects of predicate logic paradigm on *explanatory theories of reference*, and not on its merits generally.[12]

Translations of natural language sentences into predicate logic foster the compositional goal of the predicate logic paradigm because they provide a clear and systematic analysis of the combination of the meanings of the parts of a sentence into the meaning of the whole. Translation, however, aims at expressions equivalent to natural language sentences, and not at entities and mechanisms underlying those sentences. There is no reason to expect translations to achieve more than their explicit goal of equivalent expressions.[13] This point about translations does not depend upon the target language into which the translation is made: it doesn't matter whether the target language is matrix theory or Polish. That the target language is predicate logic, however, raises additional problems for explaining reference. Even though predicate logic functions mainly as a specificatory device within the predicate logic paradigm, it also supplies a mechanism used to explain reference, namely, predication.[14] Predication is used to define 'denotation': a term denotes whatever it is truly predicated of, or for singular reference, whatever it uniquely describes. Philosophers working within the predicate logic paradigm have used denotation to connect referents not only with REs that are definite or indefinite descriptions, but also with indexicals and proper names. But there are problems in using denotation as a mechanism of reference. Saul A. Kripke (1980) and Keith Donnellan (1970) have argued that proper names do not function as true descriptions of their referents.[15] In chapters 2 through 5, I argue that unique description is not the mechanism underlying either indexical reference or certain types of uses of definite and indefinite descriptions.

The focus on compositionality of meaning in the predicate logic paradigm also hinders the search for entities and mechanisms underlying reference. This focus makes truth conditions for sentences the paramount issue, so that questions about reference are treated in a top-down manner, that is, truth conditions are intuited for sentences, and the reference of an RE in them is simply whatever will help produce those truth conditions. This top-down approach ignores bottom-up considerations that are essential to an explanation: these include the actual functioning in communication of REs in relation to actions and context.

In addition to hindering the development of explanatory theories of reference, the top-down approach to reference makes specificatory theories of reference impossible. Arguments for the latter point have been given by two of the most prominent scholars working within the predicate logic paradigm, W. V. Quine and Hilary Putnam. Quine (1960, 1969) argues that reference is inscrutable on the grounds that the same truth conditions can be assigned to sentences despite differing assignments of referents to terms. This entails that reference is not specified by specifying truth conditions for sentences. Putnam (1981) develops a related argument for model-theoretic semantics. I take Quine's and Putnam's arguments to show that purely top-down theories which take truth conditions of sentences as the sole determiners of reference fail to specify reference. I propose that additional bottom-up theories may help to specify reference. And surely a bottom-up approach is needed for finding an explanatory model of the conditions underlying reference.

Yet another obstacle to the development of explanatory models for reference is the requirement that semantics is to be separated from pragmatics. These two are distinguished (in a tradition stemming from Charles W. Morris (1938) and Yehoshua Bar-Hillel (1954)) as follows: pragmatics treats the relations of symbols, objects, people and contexts, whereas semantics omits the latter two factors, and studies only the relations of symbols to objects. In practice, however, pragmatics is often defined negatively, as meaning which is not syntactical and not semantical. Like many negatively defined things, it has heterogenous components. It includes not only the reference of indexicals but also speech acts (e.g., the issue of whether a use of a sentence expresses an assertion, a command, or a question). In addition, it includes issues about communication generally, and about Gricean conversational implicatures (inferences based on rules of cooperation in conversation, which come into play after semantic content has been determined).

Associated with the distinction between semantics and pragmatics is an assumption that semantics is more important, and that pragmatics can be set aside while one works on semantics. Some philosophers apply this to reference, and assume that semantic reference can be treated independently of the pragmatics of reference, and that data from communication are not to be used for theories of reference.[16]

Are my models for reference a part of pragmatics? I don't view them in that way, because I do not accept the a priori distinction between semantics and the pragmatics of reference. Before we study the phenomena of language empirically, we do not know either the content of the theories of language or the divisions of these theories. Ptolemaic astronomy would have been an adequate specificatory theory but a false explanatory theory if it was limited to the fixed stars. An a priori constraint which separates fields of study may get in the way of cutting nature at the joints.

The a priori separation of semantics and pragmatics affects not only the content of theories but also the availability of evidence. Communication is the main source of evidence for a bottom-up account of reference, but separating semantics from pragmatics restricts this evidence to pragmatics. This unavailability of bottom-up evidence for reference in semantics reinforces the top-down approach of truth-conditional semantics.

The discipline of artificial intelligence has moved away from the separation of syntax, semantics, and pragmatics because programs based on this separation did not run. One move was to adopt theories based on Charles J. Fillmore's (1968) case grammar. These theories use schemas or frames which combine syntactical and semantical features of meaning. Another move was to combine semantics with pragmatics, for example, by including within representations of meaning both default conditions based on what usually happens, and background or contextual knowledge.[17]

In philosophy, the separation of semantics and pragmatics has led to splitting apart linguistic and cognitive matters. This new dichotomy arises from current semantic theories of reference for indexicals and proper names, especially the direct reference theory, which takes certain types of REs to contribute only a referent to propositional content.[18] Because this restrictive view leaves reference with very little semantic content, some philosophers (e.g., Perry (1979, 1988) and Wettstein (1986, 1988) have concluded that cognitive features of reference are separate from semantic features. This new dichotomy is based on the old one between semantics and pragmatics, since the informative content of reference that goes beyond simply having a certain referent is ignored, shipped off to pragmatics, or both.

The three features of the predicate logic paradigm combine to promote certain a priori tendencies regarding theories of reference, especially in regard to reference as *social* and *perceptual*. The separation of semantics from pragmatics, by removing the study of communication from semantics, also removes the most obvious data about social and perceptual features of reference. The emphases on translations into predicate logic and on truth conditions also direct attention away from social and perceptual matters. And predicate logic suggests no likely representations for either social or perceptual features. In addition, a top-down approach that focuses on truth conditions for sentences is likely to miss the bottom-up role of perception in reference.[19] These a priori obstacles to seeing reference as perceptual and social are, in my opinion, of the highest importance, since I take the most basic cases of reference, and the simplest cases to model, to be both social and perceptual.

Even if I cannot use predicate logic to discover models for reference, couldn't I at least reexpress my theories in it? Saul A. Kripke (1980: 88, note 38), who refers to Robert Nozick in the following passage, seems to think so, at least for proper names:

> . . . There is a sense in which a description theory must be trivially true if any theory of the reference of names, spelled out in terms independent of the notion of reference, is available. For if such a theory gives conditions under which an object is to be the referent of a name, then it of course uniquely satisfies these conditions.

The point here is that one can use any theory of reference as a basis for conditions whose satisfaction indicates the referent of a name. This is incorrect for an explanatory theory of reference, because such a theory does not determine particular outcomes by itself, but only in combination with subsidiary theories which allow precise calculations of initial conditions.[20] In the sciences, explanatory models are usually found long before their precise applications to the relevant initial conditions are possible. For instance, we have great explanatory models for weather, but characterizing and computing precisely the relevant initial conditions are currently beyond us, with well known results for weather predictions.[21] Because of this, we cannot restate our theory of weather in terms of necessary and sufficient conditions for particular instances. Therefore, having a correct explanatory theory for reference does not imply that one can restate it in terms of necessary and sufficient satisfaction conditions for reference.[22]

If one could deal with initial conditions precisely, then one could rephrase a non-description theory of reference into a predication theory (one which works via true descriptions of the referent). However, such a theory would still have two extremely important limits. First, such re-expression of a theory will produce a theory that is specificatory and not explanatory. This is because (*ex hy-*

pothesi) the predicate logic devices used in the new theory do not play a basic role in the conditions underlying reference. Second, even if the predication theory can express a (specificatory) theory of reference that is already known, this does not show that the predication theory would be of any help in discovering yet unknown theories of reference. This heuristic point is of the utmost importance in my present work. In my opinion, predicate logic presents a heuristic obstacle to theories of reference; because it offers only one mechanism for reference, the focus of discussion shifts from how reference works in natural language to how reference is to be represented in the predicate logic notation. This orientation distracts one from imagining new models for reference.

If the predicate logic paradigm is not conducive to explanatory models for reference, what paradigm is? How can we get at the underlying conditions and mechanisms of reference? I use what I call the '*communicational paradigm*.' This paradigm has two central features: (*a*) the goal of devising *explanatory models*, and (*b*) an emphasis on *data from communication*. Explanatory models for reference require finding simplified abstracted versions of the entities and mechanisms which underlie (either constitute or cause) the phenomena of reference. Underlying conditions and mechanisms provide a bottom-up account of reference, and not merely a top-down account based on truth conditions of sentences. In laying out these underlying factors, the models abstract from and simplify the blooming buzzing confusion of natural language use. This simplification does not make the models less empirical, since all their ingredients are empirically supported. Such simplified models are likely first steps towards understanding how reference works.

To find underlying conditions requires more than finding truth-conditionally equivalent statements. Translation, then, because it aims at such equivalence, is not a useful tool in developing explanatory models. Because equivalence is not the goal, neither are analyses in terms of necessary and sufficient truth conditions. Nevertheless, explanatory models do yield analyses of the ingredients that enter into a phenomenon. Such analyses differ from truth-conditional analyses, and instead are like chemical analyses. Consider the parallel: water is chemically analyzed into hydrogen and oxygen, and table salt into sodium and chlorine. However, a list of the elements that go into water and table salt does not constitute their chemical explanation. Also required are the mechanisms by which the elements constitute the compounds: for water, the mechanism of chemical bonding is electron sharing between hydrogen and oxygen, whereas for table salt, the mechanism is electrical attraction between sodium ions and chlorine ions. The mechanisms plus the chemical analysis constitute the chemical explanation.

The point of this parallel between chemical explanations and explanations of reference is twofold. First, the analyses that result from the explanatory models for reference provide ingredients that constitute the phenomenon, rather than expressions equivalent in meaning or extension to the phenomenon. Second, the analyses list the ingredients in reference, but the mechanisms by which those ingredients constitute reference are not part of the list, and instead are described elsewhere. Both the ingredients and the mechanisms are needed for an explanatory model.

Explanatory models must be based on appropriate data. Where are such data found for models of reference? The main source is acts of *communication*, in which speaker and hearer use words, gestures, and context to refer and to understand reference. Thus, the two central features of the communicational paradigm are closely connected: the goal of explanatory models requires a prominent place for data from communication.

An emphasis on communication has important corollaries which I view as naturally associated with the communicational paradigm, though not absolutely required by it. Foremost of these is an impetus toward a social-psychological model, rather than an individualistic one. The data from communication suggest ingredients for the models, and these data involve interactions between speaker and hearer. My social-psychological approach to reference fits well with Noam Chomsky's view that linguistics is a part of social psychology. The data from communication also suggest a role for physical objects in the models. The presence of conversers and physical objects in the models makes them fit well with Tyler Burge's (1979, 1986, 1990) recent arguments against individualism in philosophy of mind. Evidence from communication also suggests *perception* as a key ingredient in indexical reference.

Besides suggesting models, the communicational paradigm also fosters naturalism. Naturalism in philosophy has three requirements: an empirical rather than a priori approach to theorizing, the avoidance of other-worldly entities in hypotheses (e.g., Platonic forms, Fregean senses, or possible worlds construed as ontologically fundamental), and a coherence with the sciences in content and method.

Empirical data from communication have primacy of place in the communicational paradigm, and such data are large in quantity, public, and not inscrutable. It seems obvious to me, as it does to Howard K. Wettstein (1989), that it is easier to start theorizing about reference with something public and social, rather than with private thoughts inside the mind.[23] Also, the communicational paradigm avoids a priori commitments to formalisms, or to separating semantics and pragmatics; in these matters it is relatively more empirical than the predicate logic paradigm. At the present stage of development for theories of reference, it would be happenstance to find a formalism that works for reference. In general, we cannot know which formal system is appropriate to a field of study until we have some knowledge of the important parameters in that field, and of relationships of those parameters.[24] The present study aims at finding some parameters and relationships for a theory of reference.

The communicational paradigm sustains naturalism in yet other ways. The entities hypothesized in my models closely resemble ingredients in communication, so that they are this-worldly rather than other-worldly. In addition, the communicational paradigm aims at continuity with the sciences in a general way by aiming at explanatory models, and in more particular ways by utilizing notions and findings from psychology, artificial intelligence, and linguistics.

Although the communicational paradigm is constrained to seek explanatory models, and to treat data from communication as primary, in most other matters it is wide open to data and to theories, including hypotheses based on predication, perception, or social interactions.

What would success look like under the communicational paradigm for reference? Its test for explanatory models is that of the sciences, namely, checking their explanatory and predictive power. Gilbert Harman's (1973) notion of the best *total* explanatory account is important here: these models should contribute to explaining phenomena found in communication and in logical intuitions for all linguistic contexts, as contrasted to explaining only a limited range of phenomena while omitting others as has often been done in philosophy of language. Among the phenomena set aside by various approaches to language are contextual dependencies of language, cognitive aspects of language, and certain linguistic structures, such as existence claims or contexts of propositional attitude. I am not claiming that I discuss all possible phenomena of reference, but rather that they are all relevant to the acceptability of my models.

If a model for reference can explain the phenomena of communication, logic, and linguistics which prompted its introduction, it has some success. If its explanatory powers extend beyond those phenomena, this is stronger support. In this regard, I will argue that the models I use to explain the referential functioning of indexicals and descriptions also provide explanations for traditional problems about reference such as reference to the nonexistent, the informativeness of identity statements, and referential opacity. Whether the models are also explanatorily fruitful for other kinds of phenomena, as in philosophy of mind, philosophy of science, artificial intelligence, psychology, or linguistics, only time will tell.[25] I take such fecundity to be the main mark of a good explanation.

Chapter 2

Indexicals and Two Models for the Determination of Reference

I. Introduction

Indexicals are a good place to begin an empirical study of reference, because their connection with referents is open to public inspection. By indexicals, I mean terms like 'I,' 'you,' 'now,' 'this,' and so forth.[1] For example, I am going for a walk through the countryside with a friend. We are walking past a fenced in yard in which a large black dog is running along the other side of the fence and barking at us. I say, while pointing at the dog,

1. "That dog is dangerous."[2]

Ingredients in this example, in addition to the conversers, are an indexical term, 'that,' a descriptive term, 'dog,' a gesture of pointing by the speaker, and the presence of the referent, the dog, in the context. Just how these ingredients interact so as to enable the hearer to discern the referent is the main question of this chapter. This question is empirical; all these factors, their interactions, and their results for communication and logic are observable. I will offer a model for the functioning of the ingredients in indexical reference, and argue that this model fits our knowledge about communication and our logical intuitions.

The defining characteristic of indexical reference is its *dependence on the context*. Since the context of indexical reference clearly interacts with uses of indexicals and their accompanying gestures and descriptions, a model of indexical reference must lay out the roles of all these factors. In this chapter, I ask only how these factors *determine* the referent, and put aside issues other than the determination of reference.[3]

Some clarification of the notion of the *determination* of reference is needed. Determination by linguistic conventions is my main interest. However, these conventions are used by both the speaker and hearer in communication. Although both use the indexical conventions, they are more accessible in the hearer's application of them to discourse, gestures, and context, than in the speaker's application of them to his referential intentions. Therefore, I emphasize communication and the hearer's determination of indexical reference.[4]

Even though I believe that conventions underlying indexical reference can be found, I do not hold that they are available to introspection or that people are aware of them.[5] They are not rules that people consciously follow, but instead are regularities that show up in what people do. A parallel is walking: people have the skills needed for walking without explicit knowledge of the principles involved. Similarly, people develop skills of discerning and making indexical reference, and basic to these skills are regular ways of acting, which can be described in a model.

II. Two Models for the Determination of Indexical Reference

A. *The Predication Model*

On the predication model, a thing is the referent of an indexical 'that F' just in case it is the one and only F.[6] The predication model is a social-psychological model, according to which descriptions determine indexical reference in virtue of being (uniquely) true of the referent. In this model, descriptions function intellectually rather than perceptually. A hearer is to take descriptions associated with indexicals to *denote* the referent, that is, to be true of the referent and of nothing else. The root of this model is grammatical, namely, the role of predicates in grammar.

An impetus to the development of the predication model is found in Gottlob Frege's and Bertrand Russell's use of predicate logic as a tool of analysis. In Russell's celebrated paper, "On Denoting," he used a *predication* model for reference made by means of definite descriptions, but he did not apply this model to indexical reference, which he instead explained by a *perceptual* model, as we will see later. More recently, W. V. Quine continues the tradition of using predicate logic for philosophical analysis, and holds that all referring expressions are to be reparsed as predicative expressions in the predicate calculus:

Thus winnowed, what does canonical notation contain? Those of its sentences that contain no sentences as parts are composed each of a general term, without recognized internal structure standing in predicative position complemented by one or more variables. That is, the atomic sentences have the forms 'Fx,' 'Fxy,' etc. (1960: 186).

Though Quine often says that bound variables are the only referring expressions on his analysis of language, he analyzes English referring expressions (I will use 'RE' for short) by means of a propositional function of the form 'Fx' (etc.), so that all English REs are analyzed by means of a predicate plus a variable that is to be bound if the reference is successful. Thus, Quine distinguishes between REs and their use to make a reference claim: bound variables indicate the latter, whereas propositional functions, whether bound or not, may signify the former.

Quine explicitly applies the predication model of reference to indexicals:

> Now we can assimilate the demonstrative singular terms to singular descriptions, treating 'this (that) apple' as 'the apple here (there),'. . . . In the case of 'this (that) apple' the question of spatiotemporal extent, left open by the pointing gesture, was conveniently settled by the general term 'apple'; but the same happens in the general term 'apple here (there),' for it is true only of things of which both components are true. (1960: 163)

Thus, Quine treats indexical REs as functioning in virtue of being true of their referents. Although he clearly holds the predication model, in two passages in *Word and Object*, he says things about demonstratives that better fit the perceptual model: demonstratives direct attention (1960: 102), and the contrast between the demonstrated object and its surroundings are important for reference (1960: 101).[7]

Philosophers are not the only scholars of language who accept varieties of the predication model. The social-psychologist Roger Brown talks about specific reference rather than indexical reference, but he uses an example of indexical reference. In Brown's example, a son says to his father, "Can I have the car Saturday night?" Brown (1973: 341) comments as follows:

> A specific reference such as that to the family car is a unique entry [in a file], a particular card distinct from all others on which

is entered all the information about the family car, a set of properties possessed by no other entry.

It is clear that Brown takes the reference of 'the car' in this example to be determined in virtue of a set of properties that are true of exactly one thing even though these properties are not stated in the RE in question, and thus Brown accepts a version of the predication model for indexicals.

The popularity of the predication model is not to be measured merely by its appearance in papers by scholars writing on the topic of indexical reference. In addition, philosophers who deal only incidentally with philosophy of language or indexicals presuppose the predication model not only because of the influence of Frege, Russell, and Tarski, but also because of the common use of the predicate calculus.

B. The Perceptual Model

True description, which was the central mechanism of the predication model, loses this role to perception in the perceptual model. Although various perceptual relations can be conceived involving indexical REs, speakers, hearers, and referents, during the twentieth century only one variety of perceptual model was offered, and this utilized the perception of *the speaker alone*. Bertrand Russell developed such a model, but it is limited to *individual psychology*, and lacks any account of the communication of indexical reference.[8] In contrast to Russell's model, I propose a perceptual model in *social psychology*, which assigns important roles in indexical reference to *both the speaker and the hearer*. This social dimension is an essential feature of the figure-ground model.

The social-psychological model to be presented for indexical reference is called the "figure-ground model." The ingredients in the model are the speaker and hearer, the use of the indexical term along with accompanying actions, gestures, and descriptions, and the background context in relation to which the indexical is used. I call the actions, gestures, descriptions, and context, which contribute to determining indexical reference, 'complements to the indexical.' My model describes the interactions of these ingredients in indexical reference in three steps:

The Figure-Ground Model:
(i)   The very use of an indexical in relation to the context of the discourse determines the ground[9] (e.g., the physical surroundings) which contains the referent.[10]

(ii) Gestures or actions which accompany the use of the indexical serve to narrow down the physical surroundings to a subsection which contains the referent.

(iii) Descriptive content associated with the indexical term functions as a figure which makes the referent stand out in virtue of a contrast to the demonstrated segment of the physical surroundings.

(i) THE GROUND

The main role played by the context in the figure-ground model is that of the ground which contains the referent. This role is not at all like the role of providing additional descriptions that are to be true of the referent. For instance, if I use 'that dog' in the physical surroundings of my back yard on April 29, 1989, this does not mean that this RE functions in virtue of the description 'dog in my back yard on April 29, 1989.' A predication model for indexicals might use such a description for finding the unique individual that the description is true of, but the figure-ground model does not. Instead of turning the space-time location of the referent into part of a description of the referent, the figure-ground model takes this location to be a ground containing the referent. This ground is correlative to descriptions, which yield figures that pick out the intended referent by contrasting it to the background.

(ii) THE NARROWING OF THE BACKGROUND

The first step and this one delimit the domain containing the referent, in order to facilitate the third step, the application of the figure.[11] This contrasts with predication models, which pick referents out of large domains. Sometimes the very use of an indexical adequately delimits the background so that it needs no further limiting by gestures or actions, for example, spoken uses of 'now' or 'I'; if the hearer can discern the time at which 'now' is used, or the source of the sounding of 'I,' then there is no need for further narrowing of the background. In contrast, if I use 'this dog,' and there are several dogs around, I may have to use pointing to narrow the background from which the intended referent is to be picked out.[12]

Even when it seems that actions or gestures pick out the referent, rather than narrow down the background containing the referent, in fact they do the latter. For instance, I might touch someone on his shoulder or gaze into his eyes while addressing him by the indexical 'you.' Though it might seem that these actions determine the reference, they do not do so by themselves, but rather in conjunction with the descriptive content of 'you'; different references would have been made if the speaker used the same actions with the terms 'that shoulder' or 'we.'

Although actions and gestures are the main devices used to narrow down the background containing the intended referent, descriptive factors may also have this function, for example, the prepositional phrases in 'that dog on the left,' and 'that picture on the far wall.' Descriptions can also be used to direct the hearer's attention to a thing on the basis of its location in the discourse-dependent context (e.g., 'the former' and 'the latter'), but discussion of this type of context is postponed to chapter 3.

(III) THE FIGURE

Narrowing down the background which contains the referent is important to the figure-ground model, but its most distinctive feature is the role it assigns to descriptions, that of providing a figure which enables the hearer to pick out the referent by contrast to the background. *Figure* is a πρὸς ἕν equivocal term,[13] which resembles Aristotle's notion of form: shape is the most obvious type of figure, but there are higher levels of figures that have to do with the kind to which a thing belongs, for example, wolf. Anything which is perceivable via contrasts may be taken as a figure, for example, hue, saturation, and intensity of color. Though the notion of figure is most obvious in the sense of sight, it is also clearly present in perception of objects by other senses: for example, a melody, the distinctive sound of a person's voice, or the odor of a skunk.

The figure involved in indexical reference depends on descriptive factors in the discourse containing the indexical. These descriptive factors may be present *in the indexical RE itself*, or they may be supplied by the *discourse-dependent context outside the indexical RE* (e.g., "That is at least 100 decibels."). When the descriptive factor is inside the indexical RE, it may be built into the indexical term (e.g., according to Webster's dictionary, 'you' contains the descriptive factor 'the one or ones being addressed,' and 'he' contains 'that male one who is neither speaker or hearer'). Or the descriptive factor inside an indexical RE may be separate from the indexical term (e.g., 'large dog' in 'that large dog').

The contrast of figure to ground is a wholly different mechanism from true predication. Figures need not be true of what they pick out of a ground; truth may help, but it is neither necessary nor sufficient. It is rather the perceptual contrast between figure and ground that is important, and this contrast is not directly connected with truth, as shown by the following examples:

2. That man with only one kidney is a friend of mine.

3. That man with the martini is a friend of mine.

Suppose a person at a party says each of these. In (2) the initial indexical phrase may be true of the intended referent, but useless for communication at a party for obvious reasons, whereas in (3) the initial indexical phrase may be adequate for communication in virtue of a figure-ground contrast even though the description is false of the referent (suppose the person referred to has a martini glass with water in it).

To assign perceptual functioning to a description goes against the predicate-logic paradigm. This break with tradition will be supported at length later, but I mention two brief points in its favor: first, as shown by (2) and (3), the truth of a description in an indexical phrase is neither a necessary nor a sufficient condition for successful communication of reference. Second, the figure-ground model treats descriptions, gestures, and context within a single a coherent mechanism, whereas other current accounts of indexical reference, which assign descriptions the role of being true of the referent, have no account at all of the functioning of gestures and context.

Though Gestalt psychology raised the figure-ground contrast to prominence, my use of the contrast brings neither a commitment to associated Gestalt doctrines like holism or innatism, nor a concern for reversible patterns or illusions. Rather I am using the notion of figure-ground contrast as it appears in contemporary experimental psychology, where it is treated as a basic and pervasive feature in the process of organization that occurs in perception.[14] I am borrowing the figure-ground contrast from one part of psychology (theory of perception) and applying it to another part of psychology (social psychology of communication). The level of sophistication of the borrowed theory need not be high for the present purposes, as long as there is some usable positive content, and a clear contrast to the predication model.[15]

Notice how perceptual the figure-ground model is: the hearer is to hear or see the indexical use, and on its basis, determine what are the background physical surroundings. Then the hearer is to perceive gestures and actions, and use them to guide his perceptual attention to a subsection of the physical surroundings. Finally, within that subsection, the hearer is to pick out the referent in

virtue of the perceptual contrast, provided by descriptions, of figure
to ground.

Although the figure-ground model is a perceptual model, it
does not require that the discerning of the referent be a matter of
actual perception. Rather, the model allows the directing of a
hearer's attention to the referent to occur in either of two ways.
First, the hearer's *perceptual attention* may be directed to pick out,
as a figure out of a ground, the referent (or something associated
with it in certain ways to be specified later). Second, the hearer's
general powers of attention may be directed to pick out the referent
as a figure out of a ground. In the second case a perceptual model,
but not perception, is used in picking out the referent. Examples of
the second type of attention-directing will appear in the following
chapter. I begin here with simpler examples of the first type of
contrast.

Consider a case in which actions of the speaker complement a
demonstrative. Suppose that an art museum lecturer picks up a
painting in a gallery and holds it up in front of her audience while
saying,

4. This is an example of Rembrandt's style of portraiture.

In this case, the speaker's use of 'this' while holding up the painting directs the audience's perceptual attention to the thing in her
hands, and the discourse-dependent context ("is an example of
Rembrandt's style of portraiture") provides a figure which directs
their attention to the painting (rather than its frame or its weight).
If there were several paintings already in place on the wall of the
gallery, the lecturer might use (4) in conjunction with the gesture
of pointing at a certain one of the works. Then the pointing would
narrow down the background to a certain path or ray in the surroundings, and the figure provided by 'is an example of Rembrandt's style of portraiture' would enable the hearers to pick out
the referent from that path. A different way of narrowing the background would occur if the museum lecturer says,

5. That oval painting was completed ten years earlier than any of
   the other paintings on display in this room.

In this case, the use of the indexical determines a background
which is further narrowed by the phrase 'in this room.' In relation
to this restricted background, the figure provided by 'oval painting'
suffices to pick out the intended referent by its contrast to the
shapes of the other paintings in the room. In (5), the figure 'oval
painting' has quite a bit of content, and functions in relation to a

fairly large background. The situation is reversed in (6), where less content is present in the figure 'painting,' but it functions in relation to a very limited background:

6. That third painting from the left on the wall behind me was completed ten years earlier than any of the other paintings on display in this room.

Here descriptions rather than gestures are the main device for limiting the background, but (6) still resembles (4) in that both use a figure with not a great amount of content in relation to a highly restricted background.

The purpose of the figure-ground model, as shown in the discussion of the examples, is to explain the underlying conditions and mechanisms that constitute indexical reference. This differs from a specificatory purpose of providing analyses for indexical sentences by necessary and sufficient conditions. The latter purpose does not require explanatory mechanisms, and may instead use devices that are circular or ad hoc (cf. chapter 1 on this). However, an analysis of the ingredients in indexical reference can be derived from the explanatory model. To illustrate this, I repeat an earlier example:

5. That oval painting was completed ten years earlier than any of the other paintings on display in this room.

An analysis for the initial indexical reference in this on the figure-ground model would have this form:

5 A. That (context: C_1, gestures: G_1, figure: oval painting) was completed ten years earlier than any of the other paintings on display in this room.

I use "C_1" and "G_1" as place markers for details about the particular context and gestures that I am omitting here.[16] This analysis of ingredients in indexical reference amounts to the explanatory model minus the mechanisms. Because I usually do not deal with the details in particular examples by which we pick out real world contexts and use gestures to narrow those contexts, I will usually omit context and gestures from my analyses, and just note the figure, for example:

5 B. That (figure: oval painting) was completed ten years earlier than any of the other paintings on display in this room.

Which features of the figure-ground model are always required for indexical reference based on the physical surroundings? In particular, are the use of the indexical in specifying the background and the provision of a figure always needed? Also, is the spatio-temporal location of the referent always needed for determining reference? The question about indexical use is easy to answer. How could the figure-ground model possibly apply unless a background containing the referent is determined, and what could determine this background except for the use of the indexical? But must a figure be applied to the background in order to pick out the referent? There appear to be counterexamples to the requirement of a figure, because the term 'that' can be used as a single term RE, for example:

7. That is the Concorde.[17]

Suppose that the speaker says (7) while she and the hearer are looking toward the sky at an airplane that is producing a great din above them. It may seem that the referent of 'that' in (7) has already captured the attention of the hearer, so there is no need for a description to provide a figure so that the hearer can pick out the referent. However, even in this situation there is need for a figure. Consider the contrast between (7) and

8. That is 100 decibels.

when both are said in exactly the same circumstances. It is clear that the indexical RE in (7) refers to an airplane, whereas the one in (8) refers to a noise. This difference in reference can be traceable only to the different discourse-dependent contexts of the two indexical REs, since everything else in the two situations is the same. The explanation of the difference in reference must be the different descriptions in the predicates of the two sentences; according to the figure-ground model, each description (a part of the discourse-dependent context) supplies a figure, which directs the hearer to pick out a certain kind of thing from the background. The description in (7) directs attention to an airplane, since the Concorde is a type of airplane, and the description in (8) directs attention to a sound because 100 decibels is a measure of sound. Note that the attention-directing force of these predicate terms is not a matter of their functioning *as predicates*, because the attention-directing function does not require their truth, whereas their predicative function does. Thus, the hearer might respond to (7) by saying the following:

9. "No, it is a Boeing 747."

In this case, the reference of 'that' in (7) would have been successfully communicated to the hearer, even though he takes the predicate of (9) to be false of the referent of 'that.'[18] Therefore, indexical reference based on the physical surroundings *always* requires as a complement some *descriptive factor*, either in the indexical RE or in the discourse-dependent context, which provides a *figure* that the hearer is to use in picking out the referent from the background.

Finally, we come to the question of whether those complements which provide a spatio-temporal location for the referent are always required for the determination of indexical reference based on the physical surroundings.[19] It may seem that an a priori answer is possible here, since indexical reference is always determined on the basis of the *use* of the indexical, and this use by humans is always at some spatio-temporal location, so that the location would seem always to contribute to the determination of reference. However, even though the use of an indexical is always at a spatio-temporal location, it does not follow that the hearer always makes use of that location in computing which individual is the referent. For instance, suppose that you receive a telephone call from your best friend, and his greeting is as follows:

10. "Hello, I bet you will never guess where I am calling from."

And suppose he is right: you have no idea where he is calling from. Nevertheless you recognize his voice over the phone, so that you are able to discern the referent of 'I' in (10) without making any use of the spatio-temporal location of the referent. My conclusion, then, is that complements giving the spatio-temporal location of the referent are not required, even though they are often useful, for the determination of indexical reference based on the physical surroundings. The only factors always required for the determination of such reference are the *use of the indexical,* which determines a *ground* that contains the referent, and the *use of descriptive factors,* which provide a *figure* suitable for picking out the referent.

III. Arguments for the Figure-Ground Model on the Basis of Communication

It would be difficult to decide between the predication and figure-ground model for indexicals if one focused only on the models themselves, or on representational systems to which the models contribute. However, if one takes a naturalistic view of the models by focusing on their results for communication and logical intuitions, strong arguments can be made for the superiority of the figure-ground model.

A. Communication and Perception

On the figure-ground model, perception of the referent by the hearer is usually required for the communication of indexical reference,[20] whereas on the predication model, such perception is not required. For example,

11. That dog is dangerous.

Suppose (11) is said on one occasion to a sighted person, and on another occasion to a blind person. In both cases, the speaker and hearer are walking through the countryside, and the speaker points to a certain dog sitting quietly about fifty feet from the conversers. In the case involving the sighted hearer, there would be no problem for her in discerning the referent by means of the description 'dog' and the pointing, whereas the blind person would be unable to discern the referent given its inactivity and distance. Since the two hearers differ only in perceptual ability, perception must play an important role in the hearer's discerning of the referent. However, if (11) were analyzed on the predication model as

11 A. One and only one dog at which the speaker is pointing is dangerous,

and if the blind hearer trusted the speaker to be telling the truth, then the blind person would discern the content of the indexical reference, because he would know that the initial descriptive RE in (11 A) is true of exactly one thing. Since in the example, the blind person does not discern the reference made by means of 'that dog,' we must conclude that there is something wrong with the predication model.

A common objection to the argument just given runs as follows:

> Although there is a problem in the *communication* of reference to the blind person, there is no problem about the *determination* of reference in (11) or (11 A). Since communication is a matter of pragmatics, whereas the determination of reference is a matter of semantics, the semantics of (11 A) is unobjectionable.

This objection is defensible only for a *specificatory* theory of the reference of demonstratives, and not for an *explanatory* one. An explanation of demonstrative reference must include the role of demonstrations which accompany the use of a demonstrative, and their role is in relation to an audience. One could use a demonstrative while talking to oneself, but one would not use demonstrations with it, or if one did, their usual function would be missing. Therefore, to explain the determination of reference of demonstratives, one must include the role of accompanying demonstrations in relation to audiences, and that means that one must consider communication.

An example used earlier also shows the importance of perception in indexical reference:

12. That man with only one kidney is a friend of mine.

The use of (12) at a party usually would not enable the hearer to discern the referent, even though he accepts as true the fact that there is only one person with exactly one kidney there. The figure-ground model explains this by the uselessness of the description in the indexical RE for directing the hearer's perceptual attention to the referent in the circumstances (though such a description could guide sensory attention with the help of an x-ray apparatus). Clearly, the figure-ground model accounts for the importance of the hearer's perception in the discerning of indexical reference based on the presence of things in the physical surroundings, whereas the predication model does not.

B. Communication of Unique Reference

Both the figure-ground model and the predication model can account for the communication of the point that *exactly one thing* is the referent of an indexical; however, the predication model can do so only by using predicates containing either *indexicals* or *factors* (*proper names or descriptions*) that the conversers *need not* or *cannot know*. Obviously many indexical REs (e.g., 'that dog') contain descriptions that apply to more than one individual. Advocates of the predication model must find some way to restrict the application of such descriptions so that they apply to exactly one thing. The context might supply this restriction, possibly by restricting the domain of the sentence containing the indexical RE to things in the context of the sentence's use. However, as James D. McCawley (1979) has pointed out, this produces a bad result for sentences such as,

13. That dog likes all other dogs.

If the domain of (13) is restricted to the context of its use, and if there is only one dog present in that context, then (13) would be equivalent to:

14. That dog likes himself.

To avoid McCawley's objection, the restriction on extension should be applied to the indexical RE only, so that the rest of the sentence is not affected by it. Such a limited restriction is reasonable, since only the reference of the indexical, not that of the whole sentence, depends on the context of the particular use. If the context is to function on the predication model to restrict the extension of 'that dog' in (13), contextual factors would have to be incorporated into the description.[21] This might be done by inserting three types of expressions into the description: (*a*) indexicals, (*b*) proper names or coordinate-system descriptions, or (*c*) descriptions that do not contain indexicals, proper names, or coordinate-system descriptions. The first alternative obviously repeats the problem of how indexicals depend on context, and thus is useless. Examples of the second alternative are:

13 A. The dog between Lawrence Roberts and John Smith likes all other dogs.

13 B. The dog located at 76 degrees, 3 minutes, 15 seconds west longitude, and 42 degrees, 5 minutes, 6 seconds north latitude likes all other dogs.

The problem with these analyses is that neither the speaker nor the hearer of indexicals need know the proper names or the coordinate-system descriptions. The same point holds for the third alternative, for example:

13 C. The dog that weighs 63 lbs., 14 ⅜ ozs., and has 243,456 black hairs and 1582 grey hairs likes all other dogs.

In this case, not only are the conversers ignorant of uniquely fitting descriptions that do not rely on proper names or coordinate systems, but, no matter how much they learned about one dog, they could not establish that there was no similarly describable dog elsewhere in the universe. Our knowledge of things as particular individuals depends on perception, not unique description. The root problem of the predication model for indexicals is that it over-intellectualizes a type of reference that is basically perceptual.

C. *Communication of Which Thing is the Referent*

Knowing that exactly one thing is the referent of an indexical RE is not the same as knowing *which* thing is that one thing; the difference is between identifying a thing *qua unique satisfier of a description*, and identifying it *qua particular individual*. For example, suppose that you are at a party, and you hear a man behind you say the following:

15. "I don't like this party."

When you turn around you see several men talking together, but you cannot discern which one of them said (15). According to the predication model, you would have discerned the referent of 'I' in this example, because you discerned that the descriptive factor contained in 'I' is true of exactly one thing. However, since the hearer in this situation does not discern the referent of 'I,' there must be something wrong with the predication model. In contrast, the application of the figure-ground model to this example produces the result that the hearer fails to discern the referent of 'I' because he cannot pick out which of several men in the background spoke. In other words, he fails to pick out the referent as contrasted to its background.

This example not only shows the superiority of the figure-ground model to the predication model, it also illustrates a difference between the figure-ground model and a weaker perceptual model: the figure-ground model requires that the hearer perceive the referent as distinct from other things,[22] whereas a weaker perceptual model might require merely that the hearer perceive the referent.

The distinction between identifying the referent *qua* unique satisfier of a description and identifying it *qua* particular also shows that actions and gestures are not replaceable by descriptions functioning on the predication model.[23] An example will show this: suppose that three women go to a shopping plaza, and one has her purse stolen. Although she does not see the thief, her companions do, and one points at the thief and says,

16. "That man took your purse."

However, because the plaza is crowded, the victim cannot follow her friend's pointing. The third woman does follow the pointing, and she tells the theft victim that exactly one man was pointed out by the speaker of (16). Since the victim knows on good grounds that her friends are telling the truth, she thereby knows the truth of the following:

16 A. The one and only one man at whom the speaker of this sentence is pointing took your purse.

But since (16 A) includes the predication model analysis for 'that man,' it follows that the victim has discerned the referent of 'that man' as analyzed on the predication model. Intuitively, however, she has not discerned this referent. In contrast, on the figure-ground model, the victim of the theft does not discern the reference of 'that man' because she does not follow the pointing by the speaker and does not pick the referent out of the background. Thus, the figure-ground model does not allow the actions and gestures to be converted into uniquely satisfied predicates.

D. *The Roles of Uttering and of the Context in Communication*

Yet more empirical evidence from communication for the figure-ground model is found in the roles played by uttering indexicals and by the context. It is generally agreed that indexical reference is context dependent, and that the uttering of an indexical determines the context. But how does this uttering determine the context? On the figure-ground model, uttering an indexical directs the hearer's *perceptual* attention to the context, but such a perceptual role is unlikely on the predication model. However, if one attempts to use a description of the uttering as part of the analysis of indexical reference, the results are bad. Consider an example:

17. I want to leave.

If the uttering of (17) is treated as functioning in virtue of true description, the result is:

17 A. The present basic source of the use of 'I' as determined in part by the sounds of this uttering of 'I' wants to leave.

In forming a description of the uttering, (17 A) uses an indexical ('this uttering of 'I') and thus begins a regress. The way to avoid the regress is to take the uttering to function perceptually in determining the background context.

Just as it is impossible to have the role of uttering an indexical be performed by true predication, so also it is impossible to have the role of the context be performed by true predication. For example, suppose that I say,

18. "Those ducklings first showed up here about two weeks ago."

while pointing to some ducklings in my front yard on June 3, 1989. If the role of the context is that of becoming part of a description that is uniquely true of the referent, then (18) should be analyzed as the following:

18 A. The ducklings at which I am pointing and which are in my front yard on June 3, 1989 first showed up here about two weeks ago.

The description of the context still contains an indexical term, 'my'; also, the hearer need not know that it is June 3, 1989 in order to discern the referent of 'those ducklings' in (18). In contrast, on the figure-ground model, the hearer uses the context of (18) in a perceptual way.

E. A Guided Search

When a speaker makes an indexical reference, the hearer does not match the indexical RE to a list of things in the surroundings, but instead uses the actions and descriptions accompanying the RE to *guide* his attention to the referent. The predication model provides no such guidance; instead, it calls for matching the description (e.g., 'man with the martini') with all the things in the physical surroundings. Clearly, the speed with which we discern the referents of indexicals requires the search to be guided. Therefore, the figure-ground model is preferable to the predication model because only the former provides means for guiding the search.[24]

F. Summary of Arguments Based on Communication

These arguments show the importance of the hearer's perception in discerning indexical reference based on the physical surroundings. The surroundings do not function as *part of a description which fits the referent*, but rather as *a background which contains the referent*. Gestures and descriptions used in indexical reference direct the hearer's perceptual attention to pick out the referent as a figure out of a ground. Such functioning of gestures, descriptions, and the physical surroundings accounts for three important features of indexical reference: the uniqueness of the referent, the hearer's discernment of which thing is the referent, and the guidance of the hearer's search for the referent.

IV. Arguments for the Figure-ground Model on the Basis of Intuitions about the Logic of Indexicals

The underlying perceptual nature of indexical reference affects not only communication but also logic. The effects are discernible in both modal and non-modal contexts. I begin with the latter, dividing the examples into (A) those in which the indexical has a referent and (B) those in which it lacks a referent; then I take up (C) indexicals in modal contexts.

A. Non-Modal Contexts in Which the Indexical Has a Referent

There are two closely related sorts of situations in which the predication model and figure-ground model have clearly different results for the logic of propositions containing indexicals which have referents. First is the case in which the predicate of a sentence is an important part of the complement that determines the reference of an indexical subject, for example:

19. That is deafening.

Suppose that (19) is said as a jet zooms by at low altitude. In order to count the predicate of (19) as contributing to the determination of the reference of the subject term, the advocate of the predication model must analyze (19) as the following:

19 A. There is one and only one deafening noise and it is deafening.

The redundancy of this analysis was not apparent in the original, although (19 A) is clearly not tautologous because of the existence claim. According to the predication model, if the subject term has a referent, then the proposition must be true; however, in (19) it seems possible that the subject term might have a referent even though the proposition is false. For instance, suppose that one replies to (19) as follows:

20. No, that sound is well below the level that would cause deafness.

The speaker of (20) clearly discerns the referent of the indexical in (19), but is unwilling to grant the truth of (19). The figure-ground model provides an account of how this might happen. One would use the predicate term 'deafening' to supply a figure for picking out the loud noise as the referent. But even though 'deafening' provides a satisfactory figure for picking out the referent, the speaker of (20) is unwilling to concede that 'deafening' taken as a predicate is true of the referent. Therefore, the figure-ground model, but not the predication model, can explain how (19) can have a referent for its subject term even if (19) is false.[25]

The figure-ground model also works better for cases of (merely) apparent contradictions involving indexicals, for example:

21. That beautiful woman is not a woman.

On the predicational model, (21) is analyzed as

21 A. There is one and only one beautiful woman [obviously, further descriptions have to be added here to secure uniqueness], and she is not a woman.

But (21 A) is clearly self-contradictory. However, suppose that (21) is uttered at a bar that the conversers know to be frequented by transvestites. On the figure-ground model, the description 'beautiful woman' can function to direct the hearer's perceptual attention to a figure in contrast to the background, without requiring the presupposition that the description is true of the referent. Advocates of the predication model would object that this is a matter of the pragmatics of error: the hearer corrects for the error in the speaker's information, in order to form the correct description which does fit the referent (e.g., 'the person who looks like a beautiful woman'). But this response begs the question by supposing that such descriptions in fact do work in virtue of being true of the referent. Moreover, because the hearer figures out the corrected description only after he has discerned the referent, the corrected description cannot be the means by which he discerns the referent.[26]

B. Non-Modal Contexts in Which the Indexical Lacks a Referent

The predication model requires that complements to indexicals be analyzed as predicates, but does not require, *qua* predication model, either the presence or absence of an existential quantifier in the analysis. It is Russell's theory of descriptions that requires that an existential quantifier be present in the analysis of definite descriptions, and advocates of the predication model for indexicals have assimilated them to Russellian descriptions. Whether or not an existential quantifier should be used in the predication model for indexicals is a problem. Consider the following example, and predication model analyses for it (A) with an existence claim and B) without such a claim:

22.   You are the person being addressed.

22 A.   There is one and only one person being addressed by the present discourse and he is the person being addressed.

22 B.   Whoever is the one and only person being addressed by the present discourse is the person being addressed.

On the supposition that 'you' lacks a referent, the (A) analysis is false while the (B) analysis is true. Taking (22) to be true in this case is surely objectionable because of the reference failure of the use of 'you.' Therefore, the (A) analysis seems preferable.

Next consider:

23.   Who is that tall person over there?

23 A.   There is one and only one tall person over there, and who is she?

23 B.   Who is whoever is the one and only tall person over there?

Here, the (B) version seems preferable because it retains the status of (23) as a pure question, whereas the (A) version changes (23) into a conjunction of an assertion and a question. Also, if there were no tall person (or more than one tall person) in the direction indicated by the speaker, then an appropriate reply to the (A) analysis of (23) would be "That is false"; since this reply is intuitively inappropriate, it seems that (23 B) is the better analysis of (23). These examples (22) and (23) show that the predication model does not motivate the presence or absence of an existential quantifier ranging over the description, but instead this question is settled in an ad hoc manner.

The figure-ground model avoids these problems about the existential quantifier, and provides a uniform account of (22) and (23) as follows:

22 C.   This (figure: person being addressed by the present discourse) is the person being addressed.

23 C.   Who is that (figure: tall person) over there?

The descriptions in parentheses are figures which function by directing the hearer's perceptual attention to the referent. If the attention directing does not pick out a referent, the figure cannot fulfill its function, and there will be a resultant gap in the proposition. In (22), this gap results in the absence of a topic about which a comment might be made, so that (22) cannot be either true or false.[27] Intuitively, this result is preferable to viewing (22) as false in the circumstances, because informing a nonexistent addressee that he is being addressed is nugatory rather than false.

If a gap, parallel to the one in (22), appears in (23), a defective question results because the topic about which the question is asked simply does not exist. Thus, the figure-ground model would explain in a non-ad hoc way how (23) is defective without the objectionable result of including an assertion of the existence of the tall person.

Another ad hoc feature tacked on to the predication model analysis of indexicals concerns the kind of scope to be given to an existential quantifier. Suppose that a passenger on a small plane opens the cockpit door an inch or two and shouts the following:

24. "You are a skilled pilot."

Suppose also that the pilot had bailed out of the plane about a half hour before, and there was no one other than the speaker in the plane when (24) was said. A moment later the plane lunges downward, and the passenger says,

25. "It is false that you are a skilled pilot."

The alternative analyses of (25) on the predication model are:

25 A. There is one and only one person being addressed by the present discourse, and it is false that he is a skilled pilot.

25 B. It is false that there is one and only one person being addressed by the present discourse, and he is a skilled pilot.

When wide scope is given to the existential quantifier, as in (25 A), (25) turns out to be false in the circumstances given. However, with narrow scope for the quantifier, as in (25 B), (25) turns out to be true in these circumstances. Since (25) is obviously not true in the given situation, (25 A) with wide scope is obviously preferable to (25 B). But this preferability derives from the results of the analysis rather than from underlying theoretical factors, so that the choice of wide scope for the existential quantifier is ad hoc. In contrast, the figure-ground model prevents the truth of this use of (25) in a non-ad hoc way, as shown in the following:

25 C. It is false that this (person being addressed in the present discourse) is a skilled pilot.

On the figure-ground model, (25 C) would be lacking in truth value on exactly the same ground as (24) and (22): the indexical fails to provide a topic about which the comment might be either true or false.

One might object to the figure-ground model on the grounds that some propositions in which an indexical lacks a referent are intuitively false, for example:

26. In order to pass your driving test, you must leave a $5.00 bill in the tray of that money changing machine just inside the front door.

Suppose that (26) is asserted by the speaker because he sees an angular depression in the wall next to the door that looks to him just like a money changing machine used by driving examiners in the speaker's home town to collect bribes. But in fact, there is no such machine, and the angular depression is just ugly civic architecture. In this case it seems (on intuitive grounds) that (26) asserts the existence of a requirement (leaving $5.00 in a certain money changing machine) which is not, and cannot be, a requirement, so that (26) would be false. In fact, I agree with this intuition, and the figure-ground model can account for the falsity of (26). Only when an indexical is to supply the *topic* of a sentence does its failure to have a referent render the sentence lacking in truth value. If the indexical is to supply a *part of the comment* of a sentence, then its failure to have a referent may render the sentence false on some occasions, and true on others, and perhaps neither true nor false on yet other occasions (cf. Strawson (1964)). In (26) the topic is the referent of 'you,' and the comment concerns what must be done in order to pass his driving test, namely, place $5.00 in a certain machine. If there is no such machine, then the comment asserted of the topic must be false of the topic, that is, there is no such requirement because one cannot place $5.00 in a nonexistent machine.

Suppose in the situation given for (26), another speaker were to assert:

27. "It is false that in order to pass your driving test you must leave a $5.00 bill in the tray of that money changing machine just inside the front door, because there is no such machine."

On intuitive grounds, (27) appears true, since it is the denial of the requirement asserted in (26). However, the use of an indexical RE normally presupposes the existence of a referent for it, and this presupposition is explicitly denied in (27).[28] On the predication model with wide scope for the existential quantifier, (27) would contain an explicit contradiction, the assertion and denial of the existence of the money changing machine. In contrast, on the figure-ground model, there is no contradiction because this model does not bring in an assertion of the existence of the referent. Since (27) is true in the context, the figure-ground model handles it better than the predication model.

If one considers the wide range of examples in (22) through (27), the figure-ground model with its uniform and non-ad hoc account provides for a variety of outcomes for truth values of sentences containing indexicals that lack referents. In contrast, the predication model has problems of self-contradictory sentences, non-uniform analyses, and ad hoc moves.

C. Indexicals in Modal Contexts

The figure-ground model is superior to the predication model for dealing with indexicals not only in regard to non-modal contexts, but also in regard to modal contexts. For the latter, the figure-ground model explains the origins of rigidity of designation, whereas the predication model does not. Saul A. Kripke (1980; 48) defines a rigid designator as an expression that designates the same object in every possible world in which that object exists, though he does not require that the object exist in every possible world. The point of rigidity is that an RE is taken to have the same referent (rather than possibly having different referents) in relation to alternative possible circumstances. I have argued elsewhere that in fact rigidity must be a property of *uses* of expressions rather than of the expressions themselves,[29] since even a name like 'Aristotle' is an expression which has more than one referent. Here is an example to help to clarify the notion of rigidity:

28. Moses could have been more decisive during the exodus of the Jews from Egypt.

29. The leader of the Jews could have been more decisive during the exodus of the Jews from Egypt.

'Moses' in (28) is rigid because it refers to the same individual in relation to the alternative circumstances envisaged in (28), whereas 'The leader of the Jews' is non-rigid, since it could possibly refer to someone other than Moses in relation to the alternative circumstances envisaged in (29). Though Kripke first introduced proper names as rigid designators, uses of indexicals also have this status. A theory of indexical reference should explain how it happens that the use of an indexical produces rigid designation.

The predication model by itself cannot explain why indexical reference is rigid because it treats an indexical RE as determining its referent by being true of it and of nothing else. Since such a description would in most cases (the exception is when the description gives a unique essence of the referent) be true of different things in different possible worlds, the indexical RE would be non-rigid. Something must be added to the predication model to produce rigidity; one such addition would be to restrict the functioning of the predication model to the same world as that in which the indexical is used.[30] Consider an example:

30.   If that adviser talking to Reagan had studied economics in college, the economy would be doing better.

30 A.   There is one and only one adviser talking now to Reagan in the actual world, and if that adviser had studied economics in college, the economy would be doing better.

Three objections may be made to this analysis. First, it makes use of indexical REs, 'now' and 'the actual world,' within the *analysans*, and therefore it does not account for indexical reference on an entirely predicational model.[31] Second, (30 A) involves quantifying into the modal context of a counterfactual. Third, this account is motivated only in a top-down way in that it aims at securing intuitively correct truth conditions for (30); it is not motivated in a bottom-up way by the predication model. The figure-ground model, in contrast, provides a bottom-up account of rigidity of designation results for indexicals. On this model, a figure functions in relation to one possible world only, namely, that in which the indexical is used.[32] Therefore, its referent is picked out of that world, and not out of alternative possible worlds. When the referent of an indexical is discussed in relation to other possible worlds, it is that very same individual from the actual world that is talked about. Thus, the referent of an indexical across various possible worlds does not require *reidentification*, but is only identified once.

The problem of reidentifying a referent in other possible worlds is thus a pseudo-problem,[33] which arises from beguilement by a language, the predicate calculus. Because the latter allows descriptions to function only predicatively, many scholars working within the predicate logic paradigm have thought that if a description refers, it does so in virtue of being true of the referent. Then it may seem that this must hold for referring to an individual in some other possible world also.

The present explanation of the rigidity of indexical reference agrees with Kaplan's (1989a) in not requiring that the referent exist in possible worlds in order for it to be talked about in relation to them,[34] for example:

31. If all life forms had been extinguished on earth thirty years ago, then this dog would not exist.

The reference to 'this dog' in (31) depends only on applying the figure 'dog' to the context of its use, and not on alternative possible worlds. This example, by the way, is a counter example to David Lewis' (1968) counterpart theory: on Lewis' view, 'this dog' should refer to a possible world counterpart that closely resembles the dog in the actual world, but there can be no such life form in the possible world under discussion.[35]

VI. Summary and Prospects

This chapter has taken a model from psychology of perception, the figure-ground model, and applied it to the social psychology of communication. The very use of an indexical RE determines a background which contains the intended referent, and the speaker's actions, gestures, and descriptions contribute a narrowing of the relevant background, and a figure that directs the hearer's attention in a perceptual way to the referent.

Though the arguments based on communication and logical intuitions offered in the present chapter give reason enough to accept the figure-ground model, even stronger reasons in support of it derive from its explanatory usefulness in subsequent chapters. It will contribute to explanations of the semantic ambiguities between referential and attributive uses of definite descriptions, and in explaining the causes of referential opacity and transparency. Before these applications of the figure-ground model can be made, it needs further development, which is the subject of the next chapter.[36]

Chapter 3

The Figure-Ground Model: Varieties of Contexts

I. Three Types of Contextual Containment

A theory of indexicals requires a theory of context, because indexicals refer on the basis of contexts. In the previous chapter, only the physical surroundings were treated as background contexts containing referents. In the present chapter, I extend the figure-ground model to indexical reference based on different kinds of backgrounds.

The notion of 'context' may be viewed inclusively, so that for any given conversation, there is only one context, that constituted by the people and their conversation at a particular space-time location. But because various entities constitute such an inclusive context, there are a variety of modes of containment within it. In particular, some factors come with the space-time location, and others with the discourse, and yet others with the conversers. Therefore, the theory of context that I develop concerns contextual containment, the ways in which things may be contained in a context.

The function of the background context on the figure-ground model is to contain the referent so that it is available for being picked out by a figure. This function can be performed not only by the physical surroundings, but also by the discourse-dependent context and by the concerns of the conversers. However, the simplification in chapter 2 of taking only the physical surroundings as a background context does not detract from the arguments supporting the figure-ground model over the predication model. In fact, the complexity of the threefold background favors the figure-ground model over the predication model because the figure *guides* attention to the referent. The predication model, in contrast, does not guide attention to the referent, but rather matches a description to all items in the context. Such matching becomes more un-wieldy as the complexity of the background and the number of objects increase.

Since the functioning of the physical surroundings as a ground was treated at length in chapter II, most of the present discussion focuses on the other two types of context. However, I first describe additional ways in which the physical surroundings can function as a ground: it may provide bases for picking out non-perceivable or non-present things on the figure-ground model.

Context Type I: The Physical Surroundings

In the previous chapter, the figure-ground model was applied to simple cases in which a figure is used to pick out a perceivable thing by a contrast to its physical surroundings. But there are less simple applications of the figure-ground model to the physical sur-roundings. One of these involves application of the model to things which are in the physical surroundings but not perceivable, for example:

1. This university should do something about its admission stan-dards.

Suppose that (1) is used in the library of the university. In this use of (1), the RE 'this university' directs the hearer's attention to the university in the physical surroundings of the use of the RE. Even though the university as such is not perceivable, the conversers can perceive that they are located in a part of the university; the RE 'this university' directs the hearer's attention to the university that is present in the physical surroundings.[1] Physical surround-ings include not only physical objects and the conversers them-selves, but also institutions, events, situations, and attributes of these things; these more abstract entities can also be picked out on the figure-ground model.

Indexical reference can be based on the physical surroundings not only for picking out *present* things (whether perceivable or not), but also *absent* things. In the latter case, this is possible be-cause of cause-effect relations, for example:

2. This is a wonderful author.

Suppose that (2) is said as the speaker shows a novel to the hearer. Though the author is absent and thus not perceivable in the con-text, he is the cause of something that can be perceived, the novel that is being shown to the hearer.[2]

Cause-effect relations can also be the basis for indexical reference to things which the hearer cannot perceive even though they are present in the surroundings, for example:

3. That pain will last only a minute.

Suppose that a teacher of dentistry says (3) to a student: the use of 'that pain' directs the student's perceptual attention to the pain of the patient who is being given an injection of novocain. The student cannot perceive the actual pain of the patient, since it is the patient's pain, not hers. However, she can perceive the insertion of the needle, which causes the pain, and the facial expression caused by pain. Thus, she discerns the referent of the RE 'That pain' as located within a cause and effect network even though she does not perceive the pain. Consider another example:

4. This loyalty of yours is misplaced.

Suppose that (4) is stated by an army general to an army private: the latter has barred the way of the general who is trying to enter the office of a captain for whom the private works. Although the loyalty of the private is not a perceivable thing (even by the private himself), his behavior resulting from the loyalty is. The general uses the figure expressed by 'loyalty' to pick out the cause of that behavior even though this cause is not perceivable.

The extent to which part-whole and cause-effect relationships and beliefs about them can be the basis for indexical reference is an interesting issue, but I put it aside now so that I can proceed in developing what I take to be more important issues.

Context Type II: The Discourse-dependent Context

The discourse-dependent context contains things in a variety of ways, producing not only 'anaphora' but also several related phenomena of reference. To begin with the simplest variety of containment within discourse, consider these examples:

5. John Smithvogel watches television when John Smithvogel is tired.

6. John Smithvogel watches television when he is tired.

Any indexical reference is reference to a thing on the basis of its presence in the context, no matter which type of context is involved. In (5) reference is made twice to John Smithvogel but not *as* in the context, whereas in (6) the pronoun 'he' is used to refer to John Smithvogel *as* an individual in the discourse-dependent context. Because the hearer's attention has very recently been directed to things in the discourse-dependent context, minimal descriptive features will serve to redirect the hearer's attention to it: for example, indications of gender, number, and person, which are packed into the pronoun 'he,' suffice in (6) for picking the referent out of the discourse-dependent background.

Discourse contexts may contain referents by *expressing them explicitly*,[3] as in (6) or in the following:

7. John gave me his book.

The descriptive content of 'his' in (7) provides features (gender, number, and person) which guide the hearer's attention in picking out the referent from the context. Note that in a sentence like (7), these factors would guide the hearer's attention to John as the referent in most contexts. However, if the speaker said 'his' while gesturing at a certain man other than John, and used his gaze to check on the hearer's gaze, 'his' would be used to pick out a referent in the physical surroundings. The difference is in the attention-directing that accompanies the use of 'his.'

Indexical reference to things on the basis of their being explicitly talked about in the discourse often includes more description than that of gender, number, and person: for example, in the following statement (8), the descriptive term 'dog' enables the hearer to pick the intended referent out of the background:

8. That German shepherd was chasing my cat, so I threw a stick at the dog.

Note the appearance of the definite article 'the' rather than a demonstrative in the indexical RE. 'The' is demonstrative in its origins, and still has indexical force in some uses.[4] My opinion is that 'the' is used as an indexical rather than 'this' or 'that' in cases in which the referent is already closely connected with the hearer's attention. The borderline between close and not close connections is fuzzy, but if something has been referred to recently in discourse, its connection with the hearer's attention is obviously close.

Indexical reference on the basis of the discourse-dependent context may be made not only to individuals or properties but also to situations or facts, for example:

9. John scored in the 95th percentile on the MCAT exam. I told him that that would get him into medical school.

In (9) the indexical 'that' refers to the situation of John's scoring in the 95th percentile on the MCAT exam. Note that although the indexical REs 'his' in (7) and 'the dog' in (8) were coreferential with antecedents, the indexical 'that' in (9) is not coreferential with an antecedent. Its antecedent is what the first sentence of (9) expresses but does not refer to: John's scoring in the 95th percentile. An anaphorically used indexical may refer to a complex situation expressed by many sentences or even paragraphs. Suppose that a colleague narrates at length the story of the firing of a professor by a dean and university president. At the end of the narration the hearer might reply,

10. "That was a terrible business."[5]

In this use of (10), 'that' refers to the complex situation that had just been described in the discourse.

These examples in which reference is made to a situation described in discourse are related to Gareth Evans' (1980) E-type anaphora. Here is one of his examples:

11. John owns some sheep and Harry vaccinates them.

The RE 'them' in (11) cannot be treated as bound by a quantifier ranging over both 'some sheep' and 'them,' because (11) conveys a point missed by the quantified version, namely, that Harry vaccinates *all* of the sheep that John owns. The figure-ground model accounts for such E-type reference as follows. The first clause in (11) describes a situation, and the pronoun 'them' picks out certain individuals in that situation. The situation is that John owns some sheep, and 'them' picks out the sheep in that situation. The figure supplied by this use of 'them' has two components, one supplied by the plural status of 'them,' and the other by the predicate 'vaccinates,' so that the hearer is to pick out as referents a group for whom undergoing vaccination makes sense. In examples (9) and (10), the use of an RE picks out as the referent an entire situation that was being talked about, whereas E-type anaphora picks out a group of individuals within a situation that is being talked about.

Sometimes individuals have a role within a situation under discussion even though they are neither explicitly referred to nor talked about. Such presence of objects is the basis for a third type of discourse-dependent indexical reference. In these cases a definite individual has been introduced into the discourse implicitly rather than explicitly, as in the following:

12. The newspaper was missing again today. If she doesn't become more reliable in delivering it, I will cancel my subscription.

In (12) the indexical term 'she' is used to direct the hearer's attention to an individual who was known by the conversers to be involved in what was asserted in the first sentence of (12), even though she was not explicitly mentioned there. Because of the known relation of the delivery person to the missing newspaper, the first sentence of (12) implicitly directed the conversers' attention to her even though she was not explicitly mentioned. Because of this, the pronoun 'she' plus the discourse-dependent context in so far as it concerns the reliability of the referent of 'she' as a deliverer of newspapers, suffice to direct the hearer's attention to this individual.[6]

Not only are the things discussed in (or presupposed to) discourse available for indexical reference but so also is the discourse itself and its parts. Thus, we can pick out sounds or marks, tokens or types of words, sentences, gestures, or actions, for example:

13. Stanley is a positivist, but he hates to hear that term applied to him.

In (13) the complements that direct the hearer's attention to the referent are the description 'term' and the discourse-dependent context,[7] which states that Stanley hates to hear a certain term applied to him. The indexical RE 'that term' thus has an antecedent, 'positivist,' but is not coreferential with it, and instead refers to it.

Should these three types of discourse-dependent indexical reference be called 'anaphorical?' Usually anaphora is limited to reference to a thing on the basis of a prior reference to it. This would allow as anaphora only examples (6) through (8), and rule out examples (9) through (13).[8] This issue of how to use the term 'anaphora,' however, is of little consequence to my theory. What counts is whether the figure-ground model can handle all the types of containment within the discourse-dependent context, and whether rival theories can explain examples (9) through (13) adequately.

Context Type III: Concerns of Conversers

The discourse-independent context cannot be characterized simply as the physical surroundings because there are cases of indexical reference not based on the discourse-dependent context, and yet also not based on the presence of the referent (or its parts, causes, or effects) in the physical surroundings, for example:

14. The baby likes the new babysitter.

Suppose that a wife asserts (14) to her husband while both are at work, twenty miles away from the baby. In this case, it is not the physical presence of the baby that makes it available to be referred to nor is it (*ex hypothesi*) a prior reference to the baby in the context or the presupposition of the baby to what was said before.[9] Rather, the baby is available for indexical reference because it is present in the concerns of the conversers.[10] In (14) the concerns for the baby are most likely mutual, but all that is needed for this kind of reference is that the referent be a matter of concern for one of the conversers, and that the other know this (e.g., the reference of 'the baby' in (14) would be successfully communicated even if the husband did not place the baby anywhere among his concerns, but knew that his wife was concerned about the baby).

Among concerns of conversers may be found general long-term dispositions (e.g., the speaker loves cats) as well as particular dispositions whose objects are prominent either because of long term relationships (e.g., the speaker loves his son) or because of recent events (e.g., the speaker is angry at a cab driver who almost collided with him five minutes ago).

On the figure-ground model, three conditions are required for successful communication of indexical reference to things as present in the concerns of the conversers: first, the thing referred to must be among the concerns of either the speaker or the hearer; second, this presence must be known (or believed to exist) by the other converser; and third, the complement to the indexical must provide a figure that is suitable for picking the referent out of the threefold background. These conditions were all met in (14). They are also met, but in a different way in the following:

15. The new car is great.[11]

Suppose that (15) is said by a man who has recently purchased a new car. The hearer need not care about the new car, but should know that the speaker has recently purchased one, if the second condition is to be met.[12] The third condition is also met in the case, because the description 'new car' is suitable under the circumstances for picking out the intended referent.

In both of these examples, the person for whom the referent is a matter of concern (call him 'the first person') might believe that the second person believes that the referent is a matter of concern for the first person, but this belief may be a conclusion from the

success of such reference, and is not a precondition for the successful communication of such reference.

Summary: Three Types of Contexts

There is only one inclusive context for any given conversation:
it is constituted by the people and their conversation at a particular space-time location. But because of the variety of entities con-
stituting that one context, there are a variety of modes of containment within it. In particular, some factors come with the space-
time location, others with the discourse, and yet others with the
conversers. Therefore, a theory of contexts for indexical reference
has to focus on these three modes of containment, and on the ways
in which things are available for being picked out from them by
means of figures. These modes of containment and modes of availability for indexical reference are summarized in the following outline:

A. Things present in the physical surroundings
   i.   Perceivable things
   ii. Things not perceivable or not present in the surroundings,
        but obviously connected with things that are present and
        perceivable
B. Things present in the discourse
   i.   Verbal factors (words, sentences, etc.) and actions and ges-
        tures used by the conversers in the discourse
   ii. Things explicitly mentioned in the discourse
   iii. Things not explicitly mentioned in the discourse, but pre-
        supposed in what is said in the discourse
C. Things present in the conversers' concerns independently of the
discourse, and known by one converser to be present among the
other converser's concerns
   i.   Things present among the speaker's concerns, which the
        hearer knows to be present there
   ii. Things present among the hearer's concerns, which the
        speaker knows to be present there

An interesting feature of the figure-ground model in relation to
this outline is that the model is a general device for guided
searches through contexts, so that it need not be settled which context contains the referent. Consider again example (14) about the
baby, and suppose that the parents were discussing a colleague
who was ill with the flu. This discussion might bring to mind their

child who has a cold. If they then refer to their child by using the phrase 'the baby,' would it be on the basis of the discourse (B iii) or their concerns (C)? As far as the figure-ground model is concerned, it does not matter, since the search would be in relation to all contexts. Certain types of clues, however, immediately narrow down the contexts, for instance, pointing indicates that the referent is in the physical surroundings, or use of 'the latter' indicates that it is in the discourse-dependent context.

The Psychological Bases for the Three Types of Containment in Context

The theory of contextual containment just sketched is naturalistic in that it is based on certain psychological powers of humans by means of which things are present in the background of a conversation. Because of the presence of these objects in the background, the speaker may direct the hearer's attention to pick them out. For the first type of context, the power of sense perception makes a background of objects in the physical surroundings available as things to which the hearer's attention may be directed. Though the background of objects in the physical surroundings functions as a ground relative to descriptions in indexical REs (or in the discourse-dependent context), structures within it make figures applicable to it. The psychologist James Gibson (1966, 1979) says that visual perception picks up invariants of structure under transformations in the ambient light. The following structures are involved in visual perception of the physical surroundings on his view:[13] structures in the ambient light from the surfaces, corners, curvatures, and edges of the permanent layout, the occlusions and other transformations of moving and changing things. In addition to such relatively simple structures, Gibson[14] also holds that there are complex structures in the surroundings, which he calls 'affordances.' These are invariants provided by the environment for good or ill; he holds that an infant first perceives affordances, and not separated colors or shapes. Because the affordance is an invariant combination of many variables, it is, says Gibson, easier to see than all the features taken separately. Natural and artificial kinds would also involve invariances of many variables that go together. These invariant structures are what figures direct attention to. In addition to the structures of the various particular things in the physical surroundings, there is also the overall space-time structure of the surroundings relative to the conversers; the hearer often uses this structure to narrow down the range to be searched. Thus, the physical surroundings have structures within them, which are the bases on which they can function as grounds to be searched by the use of figures.

The psychological power of humans that makes it possible for the *discourse-dependent context* to provide objects for indexical reference is memory: conversers remember recent words and gestures, as well as things discussed explicitly or presupposed in the discourse. This memory, like the physical surroundings, is structured; its structure is dependent on the kinds of things talked about, the narrative order of stories, recency of mention, and other factors. Relative to this structured memory, figures associated with indexical REs may direct the hearer's attention to pick out one thing from the background.

Structures in memory also underlie the third type of context for indexical reference, the *converser's concerns*. These depend not only on memory, but also on emotional and volitional factors which constitute the concerns. Both the speaker's concerns and his knowledge of concerns of other conversers are stored in memory in a structured way. Relative to this structured memory, the descriptive factors associated with indexical REs provide figures that direct the hearer's attention to a certain thing in his memory.

Arguments in Support of the Figure-Ground Model in Relation to the Discourse-Dependent Context and the Conversers' Concerns

The figure-ground model effectively accounts for the determination of indexical reference based on the presence of the referent in the discourse-dependent context and the conversers' concerns. Indexical reference on the basis of either type of contextual containment uses the context as a *background* containing the referent, as contrasted to referring to whatever in the universe fits a particular description. Use of an indexical signals such use of the context. Second, in such contexts, the referent is determined via a description used as a figure to pick out the referent in virtue of contrast to the background. Third, a structured background is present in both the discourse-dependent context and the conversers' concerns: for the former, the structures are in short-term memory of the discourse, and for the latter, they are in memory of emotional and volitional matters. Essential to the figure-ground model are the containment of the referent in a context and the use of a figure for picking the referent out of the context. The actual involvement of a perceptual faculty, however, in providing the background context that contains the referent is not essential, because one might use an indexical and figure to pick something out of a background of some higher cognitive level than that of perception. This is done in cases involving the second and third types of contexts, as in examples (6) through (15).

Because the main features of the figure-ground model fit the functioning of indexical reference as determined by the second and third types of context, all the arguments given in the previous chapter (except the one based on the usual importance of perception in indexical reference) apply to the preferability of the figure-ground model over the predication model. I repeat the main reasons behind these arguments briefly. The figure-ground model accounts for the role of uttering the indexical in determining the context. It also addresses how one can pick out a unique referent, and pick it out *qua* particular, and explains these features by the determination of a background, and the use of a figure to contrast the referent to the background. This model also accounts for the guiding of the hearer's attention to the referent.

II. Abbreviated Polemics

I will discuss briefly three alternative accounts of indexical reference.[15] The most enlightening and most influential recent account of indexical reference has been David Kaplan's (1989a, 1989b), which I (1993) discuss at length elsewhere. His arguments are top-down, proceeding from intuitions of truth conditions for sentences containing indexicals to conclusions about the determination of indexical reference. He uses examples to argue that an indexical keeps the same referent in relation to alternative possible worlds, and thus must determine its referent in relation to its context of use, rather than in relation to alternative possible worlds. He also concludes that indexicals have a constant *character* (linguistic meaning, which he represents by a function from contexts to contents), but differing *contents* (which he represents by a function from possible worlds to extensions, but in the case of indexicals, he suggests replacing this function by the referent itself). This last point is the central tenet of the direct reference theory: an indexical RE contributes the referent itself to propositions. I agree with his conclusion that indexicals determine reference only in relation to the world in which they are used. However, his top-down arguments do not support the direct reference theory.[16] Moreover, his bottom-up account of indexical reference has only two points: indexical reference is determined in relation to the context of use, and linguistic meaning determines indexical reference. He has no theory about the contribution of contexts or of demonstrations to determining indexical reference. Because of these gaps, his theory does not even explain how indexical reference is determined, let alone why it would contribute a referent rather than a logical complex to propositions. The two bottom-up features (dependence on descriptions and on context of use) in Kaplan's account are also present in the figure-ground model, but the latter adds many more bottom-up details about the workings of indexical reference. Because of these additions to Kaplan's account, the figure-ground model does not require the direct reference theory, and can instead take the use of an indexical RE to contribute a complex of attention directing (described by the use of the figure plus gestures in relation to the context) to propositions. Such a complex will keep the same referent from the actual world even though it is related to alternative possible worlds.

Not only is the direct reference theory inadequately supported but it has notorious difficulties. It makes identity statements semantically useless, since the referent itself is in the proposition, and it makes directly referential REs substitutable for one another *salve veritate* anywhere, even in contexts of propositional attitude, which is hard to believe. And this theory places physical objects inside of propositions without giving any account of how this is possible.

Another account of indexical reference is David Lewis' (1973) and James McCawley's (1979) salience model. Lewis originated this model for contextually definite descriptions, REs like 'the pig' or 'the table.' On this view, 'the F' denotes x "if and only if x is the most salient F in the domain of discourse, according to some contextually determined salience ranking" (1979: 348). I object to this theory because it is short on content, and false. Even though salience rankings are central to the theory, it has no general account of how to determine them. More importantly, people do not run through salience rankings in searching for the referent of a definite description, but instead are *guided* to the referent by gestures and descriptions. Consider an example. Suppose that I am on an elevator at my university with a colleague when a gorilla enters the elevator and begins menacing us; I then say to my colleague,

16. "The university should do something about its admission standards."

On the salience theory, my colleague would then process the initial RE of (16) by matching it to things in order of salience (e.g., the gorilla, the dean about whom we had just been conversing, the shaking of the elevator, my fright, and so on) until he finally arrives at the university. We don't use a salience ranking; instead we are guided directly to the referent by a description. The element of truth behind Lewis's theory is a point noted earlier: 'the *F*' is preferred to 'that *F*' when the referent has already been noticed by the conversers.

Colin McGinn (1981) views spatio-temporal relations as the mechanism for determining indexical reference, for example, for 'that,'

> The referent of a token of 'that F' is to be the first F to intersect the line projected from the pointing finger, i.e., the F at the place indicated—one might almost say geometrically—by the accompanying gesture (1981: 163).

Since this mechanism is described in terms of conditions to be satisfied by the referent, I object to it on the grounds that the hearer need not know the space-time location of the referent to discern the referent of an indexical.[17] Recall an example from chapter II: a person recognizes a speaker merely by his voice on the telephone, while knowing nothing about his location. Nor is knowing the space-time location of a referent sufficient for discerning it, for example:

17. This thing in the exact middle of the intersection of State and Madison Streets in Chicago is growing rapidly.

Suppose that you are in Miami, and (17) is said to you over the phone. Do you discern the referent? No. What (17) shows is that knowledge of the space-time location of the referent is not important *by itself* in discerning indexical reference; rather, such knowledge is important as a means to *picking out the referent perceptually*. This is how the figure-ground model uses space-time location. McGinn errs, in my opinion, in taking this partial means of indexical reference as its only basic mechanism.

III. Summary and Prospects

The development of the figure-ground model and of the three types of context focus on the determination of indexical reference. I continue to focus on the determination of reference for the next two chapters, taking up definite descriptions in chapter IV, and indefinite descriptions in chapter V. The figure-ground and predication models play important roles in models for determining these types of reference.

Chapter 4

The Referential-Attributive Distinction
in Definite Descriptions

Introduction

A widely used and widely criticized distinction in philosophy of language is one drawn by Keith Donnellan (1966) between referential and attributive uses of definite descriptions. In his first paper on the topic he draws the distinction by a wealth of examples, which suggest that definite descriptions have two very different uses. His theoretical description of the distinction, however, is sketchy. The problem is just what is going on in each of these uses of definite descriptions.[1] I aim at clarifying the conventions underlying both uses. These conventions are accessible in communication, and in particular, by a study of the hearer's discerning of the reference of definite descriptions.

I. Donnellan's Introduction of the Referential-Attributive Distinction

Donnellan uses the following example to introduce his view of the referential-attributive distinction:

1. The murderer of Smith is insane.

We may imagine two contexts in which (1) is asserted. The first context is one in which I find Smith brutally murdered. When I reflect on the savage manner of his murder and on the kindly nature of Smith, I assert (1). In this context, I am using the definite description attributively, and am asserting that whoever is the person who murdered Smith is insane. On the other hand, the same description and the same sentence may be used referentially

55

in the following context. Suppose that I am at the trial of Jones, who has just been pronounced guilty of the murder of Smith. Suppose also that I know that Jones has a history of being in and out of mental institutions, and has been diagnosed as schizophrenic, and has been sitting through the trial in a catatonic state. I may in these circumstances turn to a fellow observer of the trial and assert (1). In this context, the definite description 'the murderer of Smith' is used to pick out one particular individual.

Though Donnellan offers no theory of the referential-attributive distinction in his first paper, he does make a number of comments about the nature of the distinction, most of which concern the referential use, which he takes to be his new contribution to the theory of definite descriptions. Because Donnellan's comments on the distinction do not form a coherent theory, I organize them around four topics: (A) the role of truth and satisfaction in the distinction, (B) its relation to reference and semantic analysis, (C) the role of intentions in the distinction, and (D) ordinary language characterizations of it.

A. According to Donnellan, referentially used descriptions may work satisfactorily even though nothing (or more than one thing) fits the description used (1966 in 1977: 47). When this happens, they do not render sentences in which they appear either false or lacking in truth-value, whereas an attributively used description which is not uniquely satisfied does render the sentence in which it appears either false or lacking in truth-value (1966 in 1977: 49–50; 53, 60–61). Even the speaker need not believe that anything fits the description which he uses in a referential manner according to Donnellan (1966 in 1977: 51). However, a speaker normally tries to have such descriptions be true because normally this is the best way to get his audience to recognize what he is referring to (1966 in 1977: 53).

B. On two semantic points, Donnellan describes referential and attributive uses quite differently. He views the referential use, but not the attributive use, as intuitively involving reference (1966 in 1977: 54–55), and he takes the Russellian analysis to be approximately correct for the attributive use of definite descriptions, but not for the referential use (1966 in 1977: 54).[2] Despite these semantic differences, Donnellan says, in the same paper, that the distinction is pragmatic. In a later paper, however, he (1978) says that it is semantic.

C. Donnellan says that whether a description is used referentially or attributively depends on the intentions of the speaker

(1966 in 1977: 59). Later he (1968, 1978) takes this dependence on intentions to be the essential feature of the distinction.

D. Donnellan says that referentially used descriptions call attention to a person or thing, or are devices for getting one's audience to pick out or think of the thing to be spoken about (1966 in 1977: 46). In such a use, the speaker is said to presuppose of some *particular* someone or something (rather than of someone or other as in the attributive use) that he or it fits the description (1966 in 1977: 50, 56). This last point needs a qualification such as, 'to the extent that the speaker holds the description to fit anything,' for it to be compatible with the point mentioned earlier under (A), that even the speaker need not believe that the description is true of the referent. Donnellan gives three corollaries of the presupposition by the speaker that a *particular individual* fits the description: there is a right thing to be picked out, that it could be misdescribed, and that when someone uses a description referentially, we can report the speaker as having said of the referent that it was F, and thus, we need not use his description or synonyms of it in our report, but may instead use any terms that do the job (1966 in 1977: 53, 63–65). Apparently, none of these corollaries hold for attributively used descriptions.

These descriptions of the referential-attributive distinction fail to provide a theory of the conditions underlying the distinction, and instead raise further questions about the underlying conditions: what are intentions and how do they function in communication, what is reference, and how does a particular someone differ from someone or other?

II. A Hypothesis for the Differences in the Determination of the Reference of Referentially and Attributively Used Definite Descriptions

The interpretation of the referential-attributive distinction that I will offer may be viewed as semantic in that it results in different entailments for statements that differ only in that one has a referentially used description where the other has an attributively used one. My interpretation, however, may also be viewed as pragmatic in that it emphasizes the role of context in determining which type of reference is present. But the pragmatics involved is not Gricean because it concerns the basic functioning of descriptions rather than what follows from applying general maxims of conversation to that basic functioning. Whether the referential-attributive distinction has pragmatic or semantic status is not my concern. Instead I focus on how reference functions in referential and attributive uses.

A good starting point for theorizing about the referential-attributive distinction is Donnellan's description of it in terms of ordinary language: in the referential use, we suppose a description to be true of a *particular* thing, whereas in the attributive use, we suppose it to be true of *something or other*. Just how is this distinction to be theoretically clarified?

Could it be an ontological or epistemic distinction? I think not, because even if one uses the description 'the murderer of Smith' attributively, one is still supposing that the description is true of a particular thing. In this case, the speaker does not pick out for the audience who the murderer is, but he does speak about one person who murdered Smith. Wouldn't that one person be a particular person? To make the point generally, every *someone or other* is *a particular person*, and therefore, the distinction between someone or other and a particular person cannot be *ontological*.

Nor can the distinction between someone or other and a particular person be an *epistemic* matter, as is shown by the following argument by Donnellan (1966 in 1977: 51–52). He gives the case of the trial spectator who knows that Jones is the murderer of Smith, but who recounts the circumstances of Smith's murder, and then says "The murderer of Smith is insane," and backs this statement up by outlining reasons for thinking that anyone who murdered Smith in this horrible way must be insane.[3] In such a case, the description would be used attributively, even though the speaker believes that Jones is the murderer of Smith. Since the use of the definite description is not rendered referential by the speaker's belief that a particular individual known to him is the referent of the definite description, the referential-attributive distinction cannot be an epistemic matter.

Rather than having ontological or epistemic status, the distinction between supposing a description to be true of a *particular thing* and supposing it to be true of *something or other* concerns *how we talk about things*, or the *manner of referring* to things. We may speak generally about things or we may speak about particular things *as* particular things. If one talks generally, one does not make assertions about particular things or individuals as such, but only insofar as they have certain properties or belong to certain kinds.[4] In the attributive use of a description, one refers to a thing not merely as a member of a kind but also as the only member of that kind. Despite the fact that in such reference a thing is referred to as the one and only member of a kind, it is not referred to *qua* particular because one is talking generally about whatever may be the unique member of the kind (or unique satisfier of a description), rather than about a particular *qua* particular. In contrast, in the referential use, one refers to a certain thing *as* a particular thing regardless of the predicates that it uniquely satisfies, though one may also be interested in its satisfaction of certain predicates.

Idiomatic talk about referring to a particular thing and referring to something or other reflects a distinction in manners of referring: referring to a thing *qua* particular and referring to a thing *qua* member of a kind. But this difference in manners of reference must result from a difference in the mechanisms of reference. What might that difference be?

For referential uses of descriptions, we need a means of reference which produces particularity in the manner of reference. Such a manner of reference occurs in indexical reference on the figure-ground model. Since the figure functions by making the referent stand out in contrast to the background, it directs attention to the referent *qua* particular thing standing in contrast to the background, and this is quite different from directing attention to *whatever* has a certain property.

There must be more, however, to the referential use of definite descriptions than the point that they are cases of reference on the figure-ground model, since indexicals, including the demonstratives 'this' and 'that,' are the primary examples of the figure-ground model. How are these examples to be distinguished from referential uses of definite descriptions? The answer to this question has already appeared in chapter III. When indexical reference is made to a thing already closely connected to the attention of the conversers, the article 'the' is used rather than 'this' or 'that.' This phenomenon occurs in indexical reference to things on the bases of either the discourse-dependent context or the conversers' concerns, and also when the background containing the referent is the physical surroundings and the referent has been prenoticed. Donnellan's example of a referential use in (1) is of the last variety: the conversers had already noticed the murderer of Smith in the physical surroundings.

In order for the description 'murderer of Smith' to function as a complement to a demonstrative, not only must the referent be pres-

ent in the context, but it must also be distinguishable by means of
the figure provided by the description. The description 'murderer of
Smith,' unlike 'tall man with the martini,' or 'woman in the red
dress' does not directly present *sensible* aspects of a thing, and
therefore would not work in many contexts as a figure for picking a
particular thing out of the background. It can so function, however,
in the courtroom situation in which a person has been pronounced
the murderer of Smith, because this verdict connects the referent
under that description with the attention of the conversers. This
amounts to combining two kinds of backgrounds, the physical surroundings and the discourse. Related examples can be found in
which the backgrounds for indexical reference are the speakers'
concerns and the discourse-dependent context (respectively):

2. The baby likes the new babysitter.

3. A certain dog chased my cat, so I threw a stick at the dog.

For reference *qua* member of a kind, an explanatory model can
be based on the predication model. If a description determines a
referent by being true of it, then the description determines the
referent *qua* member of a kind, namely, the kind that the description stands for. Thus, if the RE 'the tallest male undergraduate
student at the university' functions on the predication model, its
referent is whomever the description is true of, and thus it refers to
that person *qua* member of a kind (namely, tallest male undergraduate student at the university).

However, there must be more to attributive uses of definite
descriptions than the mere presence of the predication model, as
shown by the presence of the definite article. The predication
model also determines a referent in cases in which the indefinite
article is used, for example:

4. When John is hot, a glass of beer is what he wants.

The RE 'a glass of beer' refers to a thing *qua* member of a kind, and
yet is not a case of an attributive use of a definite description. This
surface level difference ('a' *vs.* 'the') is also a semantic one: definite
descriptions that speakers use attributively refer to a unique member of a kind, even though they do not refer to it *qua* particular. To
include the uniqueness of the referent in the predication model, we
must add that reference is made to a thing not only as a member of
a kind, but also as the *only* member of the kind.

My hypotheses, then, for semantic/pragmatic models of the referential-attributive distinction are these: referential uses deter-

mine reference on the figure-ground model to a thing already noticed by the conversers, and attributive uses determine reference
on the predication model, with the added point that the referent is
the only member of the kind.[5]

These two very different semantic models for the referential-
attributive distinction are masked by the morpho-syntactic unifor-
mity of the definite descriptions. I propose the following as clear
morpho-syntactic prototypes for the semantic models:

1 DC. That (figure: murderer of Smith, gesture$_1$, context$_1$) is in-
       sane.
1 IP. Whoever is the one and only murderer (with the supposition
       that there is exactly one) of Smith is insane.

'DC' and 'IP' are syntactic abbreviations: 'DC' stands for 'demonstrative and complement' (I can think of no way to pack the prior
close connection of the referent with the attention of the conversers
into anything syntactic—this is very much a pragmatic point
about the context), and 'IP' stands for 'indefinite pronoun and individuating predicate'. Even though 'the' is the demonstrative of
preference for prenoticed referents, in (1 DC) I replace 'the' by
'that' to make clearer the point that a demonstrative is involved,
and to be uniform in replacing 'the' in each member of the distinction. The parentheses immediately to the right of 'that' indicate
the complement that goes with the demonstrative. I use 'whatever'
or 'whoever' as the replacement for 'the' used attributively because
these capture the generality of reference to a thing insofar as certain predicates are true of it.

The 'DC' and 'IP' analyses express only the ingredients in the
models and not their mechanisms; nevertheless, I will use the
names 'DC' and 'IP' (by metonymy) also for the models because
these names are brief and somewhat informative (if one remem-
bers they stand for 'demonstrative and complement' and 'indefinite
pronoun and individuating predicate'). I use these syntactically
based names for a pragmatic/semantic distinction because the
shortest titles I could derive from the pragmatic/semantic description of the models were too long: 'figure-ground model to prenoticed
object,' and 'predication model to object which uniquely satisfies
the description.'

Neither (1 IP) nor (1 DC) assert the existence of the referent of
'the murderer of Smith.' Both rather presuppose such existence in
the contexts given their use; this makes them closer to Peter F.
Strawson's views than Bertrand Russell's. However, one can imag-

ine contexts in which such presuppositions would be missing, for example:

5. Keep inside; the murderer of Smith is at the door.

6. The murderer of Smith that you think is at the door is nothing but the shadow of some clothing hanging on a clothesline.

7. The murderer of Smith does not exist, because Smith committed suicide.

The context for (5) and (6) is this: the murderer of Smith has escaped from jail; (5) is said by a person who helped prosecute Smith, and (6) is the reply. In (6), there is a referential use of a definite description, but no presupposition that it has a referent.[6] Suppose that (7) is said by an investigator when Smith's body is first found, in reply to (1) with 'the murderer of Smith' used attributively. In this case, there is an attributive use of a definite description in (7), but no presupposition that it has a referent.

III. Support for the Interpretation of the Referential-Attributive Distinction

In developing the models for the referential-attributive distinction, I have already supported them in two ways. First, these models were shown to provide an account of the difference in manners of reference, *qua* particular and *qua* member of a kind, which in turn were needed to explicate the distinction between reference to a particular thing and reference to someone or other. Second, referential uses intuitively fit the requirement, already in place for indexical reference, that the word 'the' is the appropriate demonstrative to use with nouns when the referent is already closely connected to the attention of the conversers.

Since the models for referential and attributive uses describe the underlying mechanisms of reference, which have effects on communication and logic, these effects can provide support for the models. In what follows, I argue on the basis of (A) communication and (B) logical intuitions. I also use (C) a comparison of my hypotheses to Donnellan's comments on the distinction to provide additional support.

A. *Communication*

Because these arguments have already been developed in chapter II, I give only a brief resume of them here. First, the figure-ground model can account for determining a unique referent on the basis of knowledge that people have, whereas the predication model cannot. For an RE like 'the car' to determine a unique referent on the predication model, one must use either descriptions so detailed that no one knows them, or descriptions containing either indexicals or proper names in the description. The use of indexicals would introduce a circle, and suitable proper names for determining the referent need not be known.

Second, a referentially used description identifies for the audience *which* thing is the referent, and not merely that one and only one member of a certain kind is the referent. Such identification *qua* particular is absent from attributive uses of definite descriptions, which instead identify a referent *qua* member of a kind, that is, as whoever uniquely satisfies a description. The latter kind of identification uses the predication model plus the point that the predicate is true of exactly one individual.

Third, the actual utterance (use) of a referentially used RE is an essential ingredient in using it to communicate reference. One cannot compute the reference of 'the car' unless one knows the context of its use. This requirement is built into the figure-ground model, but not into the predication model. If a description is used attributively, for example, 'the first dog born at sea,' there is no need to know the context of its use in order to determine its reference. One might have to know the context of use because of other indexicals or proper names used as part of an attributively used description, for example, 'the winner of next week's lottery,' but this requirement comes not from the attributively used description as such, but rather from these subordinated items.

B. *Logical Intuitions*
GENERALITY

Attributive uses are general, as contrasted to referential uses which are non-general. This generality enables (1 IP) to entail (8), whereas (1 DC) does not:

1 DC. That (figure: murderer of Smith) is insane.
1 IP. Whoever is the one and only murderer (with the supposition that there is exactly one) of Smith is insane.
8.   If Bond is the murderer of Smith, then he is insane.

Usually, 'the murderer of Smith' in (8) would be used predicatively.[7] Then (8) follows from (1 IP) by universal instantiation, but it does not so follow from (1 DC) because (1 DC) is not universal. The latter asserts nothing about a general connection between murdering Smith and being insane: instead it uses the description 'murderer of Smith' to provide a figure for picking out an individual *qua* particular from the courtroom background. This results in a singular, non-quantified proposition in which the predicate 'insane' is asserted of that individual referred to by 'the murderer of Smith,' but is not asserted of 'murderer of Smith' taken *generally*.

It is an interesting question whether (1 IP) also supports a subjunctive conditional:

9. If Bond were the murderer of Smith, then he would be insane.

Given the situation described for (1 IP), it seems as though there is support for (9) because the person who asserts (1 IP) makes a general connection between brutally murdering Smith and being insane: this general connection would seem to hold even in counterfactual situations like that of (9). However, there is another sort of situation in which (1 IP) might be used. Suppose that the speaker knows that Smith was murdered between noon and 5:00 P.M., and that only three people had access to Smith during that time. In addition, suppose that the speaker also knows that, as a matter of fact, each of these three people is insane. In this case, the speaker would have evidence for asserting (1 IP) without requiring as evidence any law-like connection between murdering Smith and being insane. Instead, the speaker would have as evidence a law-like principle connecting having access to a person and murdering him by physical violence, and factual knowledge of a non-lawlike sort that the only three people who had access to Smith at the time of his murder were insane. In this second situation given for the use of (1 IP), there is no support for (9) because there is no reason to hold that anyone, who would have murdered Smith in other situations, would be insane; rather the evidence was only that those who could have murdered him in the actual circumstances were all insane. I conclude, then, that (1 IP) does not entail (9) because in the second kind of situation for its use it does not entail (9). The support for (9) that appeared to be present in the first situation came not from (1 IP), but rather from a *law-like general principle*, connecting the brutal murder of a kindly person with insanity; such a principle would resemble the following:

10. Only an insane person would brutally murder a kindly person.

(10) supports not only (1 IP) but also the following stronger claim:

11. The murderer of Smith must be insane.

Either (10) or (11) entails (9).

RIGIDITY OF DESIGNATION

   Contrasting to the generality of reference in attributive uses is the *singularity* of reference in referential uses, that is, reference is made to a thing *qua* particular. The means by which such reference is made, the figure-ground model, produces rigidity of designation, as was seen in chapter 2. The figure directs the hearer's attention to pick out the referent qua particular from the background of the use of the RE, and that background is in only one possible world. Thus, the referent is picked out of one possible world only, but this same referent may be talked about in relation to alternative possible worlds, so that rigidity of designation results. In contrast, attributive uses pick out a referent *qua* member of a kind, and it might turn out that different individuals fit that kind in alternative possible worlds. Consider some examples:

12. If the man on Reagan's left had studied economics, the economy would be doing better.

Suppose a woman says (12) to her friend, and both of them have been observing Reagan talking with some advisors before a political speech. The RE, 'the man on Reagan's left,' is used to refer to a particular person, rather than to someone or other, that is, it is used to make reference to an individual *qua* particular, and thus is used referentially. To evaluate (12), one does not consider who in other circumstances might be next to Reagan and whether such persons might better promote the economy if they studied economics. Instead, this very individual specified in relation to this context is the only individual relevant to the evaluation of (12) in relation to other circumstances.

   In contrast, consider:

13. If the tallest male undergraduate student at the university had ever played basketball, the coach would try to get him to join the team.

Suppose that (13) is said not in the context of looking at or talking about some particular tall undergraduate, but rather in the context of talking about how much the basketball coach values tallness. In this case, 'the tallest male undergraduate student at the university' in (13) is used to refer to someone *qua* member of a kind, and thus is used attributively. In various circumstances of evaluation for (13), this RE would take on different referents, and thus be a non-rigid designator.

DIFFERENT RESULTS FOR CONTRADICTION AND TAUTOLOGY

In cases in which the REs lack a referent, DC and IP have somewhat different results for the truth-value of propositions containing them; since Donnellan already discussed this point, it will be discussed below in section (C). Here I will discuss cases in which DC and IP have referents; in such cases, they have different results in regard to contradiction and redundancy, for example:

14. The short fat dog is not a dog; it is a wombat.

15. The short fat dog is a dog; the wombat is in the next pen.

Suppose that conversers at a zoo use the initial REs in (14) and (15) referentially. On the DC model, (14) is not self-contradictory and (15) is not redundant because descriptions in the subject REs function as figures that direct the hearer's perceptual attention rather than as predicates.

However, if sentences have an attributively used definite description as subject, and have the same description as predicate, the result would be either self-contradiction or redundancy. Suppose an attributive use of the initial REs in (16) and (17):

16. The fattest dog in the world is not a dog.

17. The fattest dog in the world is a dog.

For such a use of (16), the description in the subject RE functions on the predication model to secure reference, and part of the same description functions as the predicate of the sentence, so that the same predicate is both affirmed and denied of the same thing. Thus, (16) is self-contradictory. In (17), a predicate is used first to determine a referent, and then a part of that predicate is asserted of that referent, with the result of redundancy. Note, however, that (17) is not a tautology, because it involves the non-tautologous presupposition that there is a referent for the initial RE. These examples (14–17) show that the two models (DC and IP) produce very different results for contradiction and redundancy.

C. Comparison to Donnellan's Comments on the Referential-Attributive Distinction

My models for the referential-attributive distinction fit quite well, though not perfectly, with Donnellan's comments on the nature of the distinction. I arrange his comments as before.

a. Referential and attributive uses have different results for satisfaction and truth according to Donnellan. On the DC model, the truth of a referentially used description is merely a nonessential means for helping the hearer to pick out the referent; this is contrasted to the IP model, where the truth of the description is constitutive of the reference: the referent is whatever the predication is true of. In the courtroom situation, a referential use of 'the murderer of Smith' could still direct the audience's attention to Jones, even if Jones were really innocent of the murder, because 'murderer of Smith' can work as a figure in the courtroom situation. A true description, however, will usually provide a better figure for picking out the referent than a false one, but the additional factor of contrast to the background is very important for the DC model.

Donnellan holds that referentially and attributively used descriptions, if they are not uniquely satisfied, have different effects on truth conditions: for attributive uses, the failure of unique satisfaction renders sentences in which they appear either false or lacking in truth-value, whereas this result does not occur for referential uses. The figure-ground model explains why referential uses do not require unique satisfaction; the description functions on a perceptual model rather than by true description. The predication model explains why an attributively used definite description, if it is supposed to supply a topic but lacks a referent, renders sentences containing it either false or lacking in truth-value, for example:

18. The grader of your examination is intelligent.

If the initial RE of (18) is used attributively, and fits no one, then (18) is defective, and cannot be true. Contrary to Donnellan's opinion, however, even an attributively used description with no referent may appear in a true sentence if the description is part of a comment, for example:

19. You don't have to bribe the grader of your written examination because it will not be graded.

My disagreement with Donnellan here is not about the referential-attributive distinction, but rather about its application to sentences. It seems that Donnellan did not consider cases like (19) in which an attributively used description is part of a comment.[8]

b. According to Donnellan, the referential use of a description involves reference, whereas the attributive use does not. On this point I disagree with Donnellan, but because my position depends on a general theory of the nature of reference to be developed in the next two chapters, I must postpone the issue. Another semantic claim made by Donnellan about the distinction is that the Russellian analysis is approximately correct for the attributive use of definite descriptions, but not for the referential use. My models for the distinction agree with this point. The IP model is closer to Russell's analysis than is the DC model, because the former leads to a general proposition, whereas the latter leads to a singular, non-general proposition (insofar as its contribution is concerned—something else in the proposition may require generality). However, the Russellian analysis includes an assertion of the existence of the referent, whereas the IP model does not, even though in most contexts (but not in that of (19)) it *presupposes* the existence of the referent.

c. Donnellan assigned intentions a role in determining whether a description is used referentially or attributively. Although I agree that intentions do have a role in the choice of the DC or the IP models, I will argue near the end of the chapter that intentions by themselves do not suffice for explicating the distinction.

d. In regard to ordinary language characterizations of the distinction, the IP and DC models fully agree with Donnellan's views. Donnellan's ordinary language characterization of the distinction, in terms of referring to a particular someone *vs.* referring to someone or other, was the clue which led me first to the differences in manners of reference (*qua* particular and *qua* member of a kind), and then to the models. Also, referentially used descriptions according to the DC model are devices for getting one's audience to pick out the thing to be spoken about; they do so by the figure-ground model.

However, the corollaries of the distinction between referring to a particular someone *vs.* referring to someone or other merit discussion. First, Donnellan holds that in the referential use, there is a right thing to be picked out: this is certainly the case on the figure-ground model, because the speaker intends in using this model to pick out a certain referent by means of the description used as a figure. In contrast, if a thing is referred to on the IP model as the unique satisfier of a description, there is a right kind of thing (whatever uniquely fits 'F') to be picked out, but not a right thing *qua* particular. Donnellan also holds that the referent of a referentially used description could be misdescribed. This could happen on the figure-ground model if the figure is not true of the referent, but still serves to pick it out by contrasting it to the background.

Yet another corollary that Donnellan draws from the point that referentially used descriptions refer to a particular someone is this: we can report that a speaker using a description referentially said of the referent that it was *F*, and thus, we need not use his description in our report. Although this corollary may be correct for reports of beliefs originally expressed in subject-predicate sentences, it does not hold for reports of beliefs originally expressed in identity statements, for example:

20. The barrel on the left is different from the barrel suspended from the ceiling.

Suppose that Harold is in a room containing many mirrors, and that he says (20), pointing in different directions with each of the REs. Suppose also that what Harold took to be two different barrels was in fact one barrel. Then I could not report what Harold said merely by saying,

21. "Harold said of this barrel that it was different from itself."

Using (21) is not a good way to report (20), because (21) reports Harold's statement as self-contradictory, whereas (20) was not self-contradictory. Therefore, despite the fact that the REs were used referentially in (20), the use of the idiom 'he said of this *F*' may result in a misleading report: apparently, the way the person refers by means of the referentially used description must be reported in this case, and not just the thing to which reference was made.

IV. Ambiguity and the Referential-Attributive Distinction

Is a definite description like 'the murderer of Smith' ambiguous? Yes, it has different meanings in different contexts, and this is the definition of ambiguity.[9] The ambiguity involved in the referential-attributive distinction comes from the differences in syn-

tax, semantics, and pragmatics which the DC and IP models clarify. Thus, the ambiguity concerns referential functioning, rather
than lexical semantics. Jennifer Hornsby (1977: 33) suggests otherwise, taking the word 'the' to be ambiguous in referentially and
attributively used descriptions, but this seems unwarranted since
the ambiguity pertains to the syntax and semantics of the entire
RE, rather than the single word 'the.'[10]

V. Abbreviated Polemics

A brief discussion of alternative interpretations of the referential-attributive distinction also supports my interpretation. Donnellan develops a point from his first paper into a semantic interpretation of the distinction in two later papers. In his (1968) second
paper, he takes the speaker's intentions as basic to the distinction,
and in his (1978) third paper, he takes the referential use, but not
the attributive, to involve speaker reference. The main problem in
his theory concerns the content of the speaker's intentions: How do
they get content, and how do hearers discern it? Donnellan's (1968:
212) answer is that a speaker's intentions are limited by his expectations, which in turn are limited by established practices and by
particular stipulations. As a parallel, Donnellan suggests that if
we ask someone to flap his arms with the intention of flying, he
cannot do so; even though he can flap his arms, he can do so with
the intention of flying only if his expectation is that the flapping
will result in flying. This example indicates that not just any expectations, but rather *rational* ones, are what limit intentions, and
Donnellan (1968: 213) also says this explicitly.

Donnellan, therefore, draws the referential-attributive distinction as follows: which way a description is used is determined by
intentions, which are limited by rational expectations, which in
turn are limited by established practices and stipulations. Therefore, to discern how a description is used, one must understand the
practices associated with both uses of descriptions. But Donnellan
does not give an account of these practices in any of his papers.
Were he to give such an account, it might well suffice for drawing
the distinction, without the need to bring in intentions.

In his third paper on the referential-attributive distinction,
Donnellan uses examples to argue that speaker reference is present in referential uses, but not in attributive uses. By 'speaker's
reference,' he means what the speaker intends to refer to, as contrasted to what the description uniquely fits. One problem in his

argument is his supposition that if a description does not determine its referent by unique fit, the only other way it can do so is in virtue of the speaker's intentions. I would object that there is a third alternative, the figure-ground model. Another problem is that speaker's intended reference can differ from unique fit also in attributively used descriptions,[11] for example:

22. The winner of next week's lottery will have to pay most of it back in taxes.

Suppose the speaker of (22) is talking about new tax laws, and believes that the winner of next week's lottery is identical with the winner of the next lottery, though he has no particular individual in mind. However, no lottery is to be held next week, and the next lottery will be the week after next. In this case, the speaker would intend his assertion to be about the winner of that lottery, since he intended to speak about the winner of the next lottery. Thus, speaker's reference is different from semantic reference in the use of (22), even though the RE is clearly used attributively. A slip of the tongue in an attributive use could also produce a divergence of speaker's intended reference from semantic reference. What allows these divergences is that there is a right kind of individual that the speaker has in mind, but he misdecribes that kind. Donnellan (1968) had mentioned the possibility of such a divergence earlier.

Both Saul A. Kripke and John Searle have devised Gricean pragmatic interpretations of the referential-attributive distinction.[12] These are based on a contrast between (A) speaker's reference, which is at the level of intentions rather than of language, and (B) semantic or linguistic reference. They define the referential use as one in which (A) and (B) diverge, and the attributive use as one in which they are identical. This account is the same as Donnellan's, except that he views the distinction as semantic because of examples in which the distinction affects the truth conditions of sentences, whereas they view it as pragmatic and not affecting truth conditions.

Because both Kripke and Searle agree with Donnellan in taking the speaker's reference and the semantic reference to coincide for attributive uses, their views are vulnerable to the same counter-example given in (22) above. Since speakers can make errors in using descriptions attributively, all three philosophers err in describing attributive uses. Therefore, I need not discuss Kripke's and Searle's particular views on attributive uses, and may focus instead on their accounts of referential uses.

On Kripke's view of referential uses, the speaker has a specific intention to refer to a certain object and he uses a description which he believes is true of that object. One problem in this view is that a speaker need not believe that a description he uses referentially is true of the referent, for example:

23. Is the king in his counting house?

Donnellan (1966) states that the speaker need not believe that the person he refers to by means of 'the king' really is the king. Kripke (1977: 273, note 22) replies to Donnellan's example by saying that it shades into ironical or inverted commas cases. However, this seems unlikely for (23), since using inverted commas around 'king,' or talking ironically about the king might be prohibited by law, but such a law would not prohibit the use of (23).

Another problem in Kripke's account concerns what he calls "indefinite definite descriptions," like 'the dog.' He (1977: 271) says that if they can be assimilated to demonstrative reference, then they would provide a new argument in favor of a semantic interpretation of the referentially used descriptions. Just such an assimilation is provided by the figure-ground model.

Searle's (1979) account of the referential-attributive distinction requires three background assumptions about reference. First, he claims that all reference represents an object under some aspect. Second, the referent is what satisfies the aspect, or, whatever the aspect is true of. Third, the primary aspect under which one refers is an aspect such that if nothing satisfies it, the statement cannot be true. Then Searle defines an attributive use as one in which reference is made under the primary aspect. This requires an identification of the speaker's intended reference and the semantic reference under the aspect, so that it is vulnerable to examples like (22) in which these two diverge.[13] He defines referential uses as those in which reference is made under a secondary aspect. Thus, referential uses allow for a divergence between the speaker's intended reference (under the primary aspect) and the semantic reference (under the secondary aspect).

Searle's account of referential uses requires that a speaker have in mind some description (a primary aspect) other than the description he uses referentially. But this need not be the case, for example:

24. The big person who is wearing a blue ski mask and is running that way just came out of the bank.

Suppose that (24) is said (with pointing) just after a bank has been robbed. Although the initial RE in (24) intuitively is used referentially, the speaker knows no other aspect under which she can refer to the referent of the initial RE, and therefore, on Searle's construal of the referential-attributive distinction, this RE is used attributively. But intuitively, it is used referentially.

A common argument in Donnellan's, Kripke's, and Searle's accounts of the referential-attributive distinction is that since a referentially used description can have a referent without being true of it, its referring function must be produced by the speaker's intentions rather than by the use of the words in the context. This argument supposes that the only linguistic mechanism for reference is true description. I have argued against this supposition at length in chapters 2 through 4. Because they view true description as the only mechanism of linguistic reference, they see the speaker's intention, a non-linguistic means, as the only way left to determine reference. But this is grasping at a straw. Speaker's intentions accompany *all* of language; if they are held to accomplish some special feat in regard to referentially used descriptions, we deserve some account of how this happens. Especially important is how hearers discern these intentions. Donnellan is the only one to tackle this issue, saying that hearers discern intentions by figuring what reasonable expectations the speaker could have, and that practices play an important role is discerning such expectations. But if there are practices regarding the referential-attributive distinction, why not use them as a basis for a semantic account of the distinction?[14] [15]

VI. Summary and Prospects

Donnellan's referential-attributive distinction can be explained as follows: in a referential use, reference is made to a prenoticed thing on the figure-ground model, and in an attributive use, reference is made to a thing on the predication model, with the added point that the referent is the only member of the kind. These accounts, like that given for indexical reference, explain only the determination of reference, and not the basic nature of reference itself. In the next chapter, difficulties in explaining the nature of the distinction between specific and non-specific reference made by means of indefinite descriptions will lead to the broader topic of the nature of reference.

Chapter 5

Specific and Non-specific Reference by Means of Indefinite Descriptions

I. The Problem of the Contrast Between Specific and Non-specific Reference.

The ambiguity between referential and attributive uses of definite descriptions seems to have a parallel in uses of indefinite descriptions. Here is an example from John Lyons (1977a: 188):

1. Every evening at six o'clock a heron flies over the chalet.

The use of the description 'a heron' in this statement is ambiguous, as shown by its meaning in different contexts. For instance, suppose that (1) is followed by:

2 A. It has a nest with some eggs under the front porch; if small children feed it, it is not afraid.

Then the reference made by 'a heron' is specific. Suppose (2) is instead followed by:

2 B. I don't know where so many herons come from.

Then the reference is probably non-specific. Note that more than one sentence is needed in this example and in most examples for the specific-non-specific distinction. Because of this, those philosophers who focus on one sentence at a time have missed the distinction. It is strange that in teaching writing the importance of discourses larger than one sentence is taken for granted, but that in philosophy of language such discourses are usually ignored.[1]

It has been suggested by Peter Geach (1962: 8, 127) that the difference between specific and non-specific reference is merely a matter of speaker's reference and not one of semantics.[2] The effects of negation on indefinite descriptions argue against this suggestion, for example:

3. John plans to marry a very intelligent woman. However, he does not believe that she is intelligent.

75

4. John plans to marry a very intelligent woman. His reason is
that he gets along well with intelligent women; however, he
plans to put off his decision about whom to marry for at least
five years.

In (3) the RE 'a very intelligent woman' is used to make specific
reference, and in (4) it is used to make non-specific reference. The
negations of (3) and (4) are:

3 N. John does not plan to marry a certain very intelligent
woman.

4 N. John does not plan to marry any very intelligent woman.

These negations are semantically different, and since the two original propositions differ only in that an RE was used in one to make
specific reference and in the other to make non-specific reference,
these two kinds of reference must differ semantically.

A second type of logical evidence for the semantic status of the
specific-non-specific distinction is in its results for rigidity of designation, for example:

5. If you were to cut three classes in a course with a certain colleague of mine, you would automatically receive an F in the
course.

In the alternative possible circumstances in which (5) is evaluated,
'a certain colleague' has the same referent, and is thus rigid. In
contrast, the RE 'a course' in (5) may be taken either as specific or
non-specific, with the latter the more likely interpretation; on this
interpretation, 'a course' may have different referents in different
possible worlds, and is thus non-rigid.

Though there is an obvious intuitive difference between specific and non-specific reference in these examples, it is difficult to
characterize this difference. John Lyons (1977a: 188) describes such
reference as reference to a specific individual, as do many linguists. However, Lyons (1977a: 178) also states that indefinite expressions do not refer to a specific individual; thus, Lyons, despite
his great skill at drawing together diverse types of semantics, is
inconsistent on specific reference. Moreover, reference to a specific
individual seems open to the same problem raised in the previous
chapter concerning reference to a particular individual: the only
individuals that exist are specific (and particular) ones. Also, the
very phrase, 'a specific individual,' need not refer to a specific individual, for example:

6. All poor teachers pick a specific individual to be their favorite student.

Since 'a specific individual' in (6) does not refer to a specific individual, clearly the intuitive notion involved in reference to a specific individual is not a matter of the nature of the referent (i.e., of ontology). Any account of specific reference must explain its similarity to referential uses of definite descriptions; both involve reference to a specific (or particular) thing.

Parallels to the Referential-Attributive Distinction

A reasonable conclusion from the similarity of specific reference to the referential uses of definite descriptions is that both involve reference in some sense to a specific thing where such specificity concerns not the ontological status of the referent, but rather the *manner* of reference. This conclusion is supported also by the fact that one can make specific reference, and thus some sort of reference *qua* particular, not only to ontological particulars but also to properties and relations, for example:

7. I have picked a certain shade of white for the kitchen.

Logical parallels between the specific-non-specific distinction and the referential-attributive distinction also support viewing the manner of reference as basic to both distinctions. *Qua* particular reference produces both singular reference and rigid designation; these appear in both referentially used definite descriptions and specific reference made by means of indefinite descriptions. *Qua* member of a kind reference produces general or quantified reference and non-rigid designation; these appear in both attributively used definite descriptions and non-specific reference made by means of indefinite descriptions. Although differences in regard to negation can be used to test (e.g., on (3) and (4)) for logical differences between singular and quantified reference for indefinite descriptions, negation cannot provide such a test for definite descriptions, because in attributive uses of definite descriptions, reference is to a thing *qua one and only* member of the kind. The uniqueness of membership in the kind makes negation affect attributive and referential uses similarly. Nevertheless, the difference in rigidity of designation between specific and non-specific uses of indefinite descriptions (e.g., in (5) the rigid use of 'a certain colleague' *vs.* the non-rigid use of 'a course') does find a parallel in referential and attributive uses of definite descriptions. Suppose that Jones has been found guilty of murdering Smith, and that the prosecuting attorney says in discussing with a colleague the prospects for the sentence:

8. "If the murderer of Smith were to ask for a light sentence because of his lack of prior convictions, I would argue that in three separate instances this lack was due to incompetent police work."

Note that 'the murderer of Smith' in (8) has the same referent in all alternative possible worlds, just as did 'a certain colleague' in (5). In contrast, attributive uses produce non-rigid designators, for example:

9. If the first prize winner of a New York State lottery received the entire prize in one lump sum, the taxes would be higher.

In the context of a general discussion of lottery prizes, the RE 'the first prize winner of a New York State lottery' picks out different referents in different possible circumstances.

Despite the similarity of the specific-non-specific distinction to the referential-attributive distinction in regard to manners of reference and logic, it is a mistake to identify the two distinctions, as was done by Barbara Hall Partee (1970). Rather, each member of one distinction differs from the parallel member of the other distinction. First, an attributively used definite description presents its referent as the one and only member of a kind, whereas non-specific reference made by means of an indefinite description presents its referent merely as a member of a kind without the added point that it is the only member (though it does indicate a single referent). An obvious difference also exists between referentially used definite descriptions and specifically used indefinite descriptions. The former purports to identify for the hearer *which thing* is the referent; consider the use of 'the murderer of Smith' in the courtroom setting of (8). In contrast, specific reference by means of an indefinite description does not purport to identify for the hearer *which thing* is the referent (e.g., the use of 'a certain colleague of mine' in (5)). Since specific reference shares one feature with referentially used descriptions, and differs on another, and since non-specific reference does the same in relation to attributively used descriptions, the most simple explanatory hypothesis for the pair of distinctions would have the following form: their members share one feature and differ on another. But what are these features?

The difference between specific reference made by means of an indefinite description and the referential use of a definite description is not one of extension, since both purport (in most cases) to have exactly one referent. Nor is it one of the manner of reference since both in some way determine a referent *qua* particular, as shown by the resultant rigidity. This indicates that there must be a third dimension, that enters into specific reference beyond the discussions of extensions and manners of reference. This third dimension is based on the purposes of reference.

II. Two Purposes of Reference: Identification for the Audience *vs.* Providing a Means for Talking about the Referent[3]

A. A Third Dimension of Reference Shown by Purposes

I propose that a third dimension of reference can be seen in relation to the purposes for which REs are used. One purpose is to inform the audience of the identity of the referent, and another is to provide a means for talking about the referent.[4] The function of identification of the referent for the audience aims at having the audience recognize which or what kind of thing we are talking about. This function differs from that of providing a means for talking about the referent, which might be done even if there were no audience. The two purposes of identifying the referent for the audience and providing a means for talking about the referent can be separated so that one is sought and satisfied without the other. On the one hand, an RE can be used as a *means for talking about something*, but *not to identify* that thing for an audience, for example:

10. I have to fix that.

Suppose that I say (10) while musing to myself, and that I am using 'that' in (10) to refer to a certain leaky faucet. In this case there is no audience, and even if there were (perhaps unknown to me), 'that' would serve as a means for talking about a thing without identifying it for the audience.

On the other hand, an RE can be used to *identify something for the audience* without also using it as a *means for talking about the referent*, for example:

11. "Horsie!"

12. "There goes a mouse!"[5]

Suppose that (11) is said to a one-year-old child: an item is identified for the audience, but it need not be talked about any further.

Adults might be the audience for (12), and it might, but need not, be followed by other sentences about the mouse. Additional cases of identifying a thing for an audience without going on to talk about it occur in the use of signs and name tags. These are linguistic entities that serve to identify people, places, or establishments without any need for going on to talk about them. Such names may be appended to the actual object in the physical world or to a representation of the object on a map, and in both cases, they identify without being used as a means for saying something about the object.

Not only are there two different and separable purposes in reference, but also there are distinct activities aimed at each purpose. The purpose of identifying a thing for the audience, is carried out by the activity of identifying a thing for the audience, and the purpose of providing a means for talking about a thing is carried out by the activity of introducing a thing into a proposition. The latter activity relates the referent to other things to which attention is also directed in discourse, for example, to properties and relations expressed in a proposition. For an initial approach to the problems of specific and non-specific reference, the notion of 'introduction into a proposition' as contrasted to that of 'identification for the audience' will suffice. However, because of problems concerning the former notion, I will replace it with a more refined notion in the next chapter.

In earlier chapters, I had talked as though the basic activity of reference was simply that of determining a referent, but now I have argued for two different basic activities within reference, identifying a thing for the audience and introducing a thing into a proposition. Each of these includes determining a referent as a part, but connects it with diverse factors, in one case a relation to the audience, and in the other a relation to parts of a proposition. Because these basic activities which constitute reference include determining the referent, each can take on the manners (*qua* particular and *qua* member of a kind) and the means (figure-ground model and predication model) of determining reference developed earlier.

B. A Difference in the Manners of Introducing into a Proposition and Identifying for the Audience

I have argued on the basis of examples (10) through (12) that the two purposes (and activities) of identifying a thing for the audience and making it available for being talked about can be separated. However, it is not usual for them to be separated; they might diverge, but to a smaller extent, by differing only in their *manners* of functioning, *qua* particular or *qua* member of a kind. Such a divergence in manners of identifying a referent for the audience and introducing it into a proposition occurs in specific reference made by means of indefinite descriptions. In such reference, the manner of functioning for *introduction into a proposition* is *qua particular*, whereas the manner of functioning for *identification for the audience* is *qua member of a kind*. In contrast, in *non-specific reference*, the manners of functioning for both *introduction into a proposition* and *identification for the audience* are the same, namely, *qua member of a kind*. In addition, non-specific reference made by means of a description of the form 'an F' requires, because of the meaning of 'an,' the referent to be a single thing even though the referent is introduced into the proposition and identified *qua* member of a kind.[6]

This hypothesis about divergence in manners of reference in specific reference fits our previous examples well:

13.   John plans to marry a certain very intelligent woman. If she and John were to take IQ tests, she would score 50 points above him.

13 A. If John and a certain very intelligent woman, whom he plans to marry, were to take IQ tests, she would score 50 points above him.

The RE 'a certain very intelligent woman' in (13 A) introduces its referent into a proposition *qua* particular, as shown by the fact that it is a rigid designator. It seems reasonable to suppose that it is also rigid in the parallel (13).[7] The logical feature of rigidity of designation derives from the introduction of a referent *qua* particular into a propositions. Despite the fact that the use of 'a very intelligent woman' in (13) produces introduction *qua* particular, it does not identify its referent *qua* particular for the audience. The audience is told the *kind* (very intelligent woman) to which the referent belongs, but not *which* individual is the referent.

There are at least three reasons why a speaker might wish to introduce a thing into a proposition *qua* particular while identifying it for the audience only *qua* member of a kind: (a) a desire for secrecy,[8] (b) a lack of ability on the part of the audience to apprehend the identity of the referent because of their lack of knowledge of the relevant contexts, and (c) a lack of ability on the part of the speaker to point out the referent because of his lack of knowledge about the referent or its surroundings. Points (b) and (c) often interact. Consider an example of specific reference motivated by (a):

14. If a certain member of our organization who has infiltrated the Ku Klux Klan were to be discovered, he would lose his job, and his life might even be in danger.

Because the RE 'a certain member of our organization who has infiltrated the Ku Klux Klan' in (14) is a rigid designator, referring to the same individual in alternative possible worlds, it must introduce its referent *qua* particular. The reason why the identity of the referent was not given to the audience in the case of (14) is that it would endanger the job and the safety of the infiltrator.

Points (b) and (c) would be involved in the following situation. Suppose that you are at a party, and you notice an old friend across the room. You wish to comment on him to the person you are now talking to, but you cannot indexically pick him out because of the crowd. You might say,

15. "If you were to be an employee of a certain man on the other side of the room, who is an old friend of mine, you would like your work."

In this case, the reference by the RE 'a certain man on the other side of the room' in (15) is specific because it introduces a person *qua* particular, but the reason why the person is identified *qua* member of a kind is that there was no handy way to identify the referent *qua* particular in those circumstances. Nevertheless, the speaker wanted to say something about the referent *qua* particular, not merely *qua* member of a kind, and he did so.

Consider finally a most important type of example, in which (c) (the speaker's inability to pick out the referent) alone is operative as a reason for the lack of identification *qua* particular of the referent for the audience.

16.   John is going to marry a certain woman that Harold knows, but that I do not know. She has been working on a project with John for two months, and they fell madly in love. If she had not had such a horrible earlier marriage, they would be married by now.

16 A. If a certain woman who is going to marry John had not had such a horrible earlier marriage, she and John would be married by now. I don't know her, but Harold does.

(16 A) is a variant way of telling the same story as (16). In (16 A), the referent of 'a certain woman who is going to marry John' is

introduced *qua* particular, as shown by its rigidity, but the speaker lacks knowledge of the referent *qua* particular. Instead the speaker makes use of someone else's knowledge of the referent *qua* particular to determine which thing is the referent. This other person's knowledge of the referent *qua* particular is known by the present speaker through some unspecified chain of discourse that probably involves Harold. This situation resembles that of anaphorical reference within a conversation, in which one speaker picks up on the reference of an earlier speaker. The parallel to anaphora shows the reasonableness of allowing such reference *qua* particular: there is nothing defective about allowing a second speaker to pick up on a prior speaker's reference *qua* particular within a conversation, even though the second speaker does not have sufficient knowledge to identify the referent *qua* particular. But if this is so, why couldn't the anaphorical chain extend beyond the original discourse, with later speakers making use of a specification of the referent by some earlier (but now absent) speaker. Such reference depends ultimately on someone's knowledge of a thing *qua* particular, even though the present speaker may lack such knowledge. This dependence on other speakers for the introduction of a referent into a proposition in the use of 'a certain woman who is going to marry John' in (16 A) shows the *social nature* of reference, and thereby shows that the falsity of what Searle (1969: 87–91) calls the 'principle of identification.'[9]

Ex hypothesi, the speaker in (16 A) cannot identify the referent *qua* particular, even though he talks about her *qua* particular. Therefore, he identifies her for the audience only partially, that is, *qua* member of a kind rather than *qua* particular. Even this partial identification of the referent for the audience seems to be based on societal factors, namely, what the speaker has heard from others about the referent. Thus, both the specification *qua* particular of the referent, and its partial identification for the audience, are based on the cooperation of other speakers with the present speaker.[10] Because in (16 A) the speaker wants to talk about a person *qua* particular, but *cannot* identify her *qua* particular for the audience, he needs to use a device which allows introduction *qua* particular into a proposition without concomitant identification *qua* particular for the audience. Clearly, the present account of reference places it not in individual psychology or epistemology[11] but rather in social psychology. Not just the communication of reference is social, but also its determination.

What mechanism produces specific and non-specific reference by means of indefinite descriptions? The answer is relatively easy for non-specific reference. It is produced on the *predication model*; the referent is both introduced into a proposition and identified for the audience as fitting the description. Also, the indefinite article '*a*' indicates that the referent is one member (even if not the only member) of the kind associated with the description. But this pred- ication-model functioning may be said to "introduce an *indetermi- nate* thing" into discourse. Such indeterminacy is not a matter of ontology since there are no indeterminate things, but instead con- cerns the manner of referring: the indefinite article plus the predi- cation model introduces a thing insofar as it has the property ex- pressed by the predicate, while leaving out of consideration which thing it may be *qua* particular.

For specific reference, the mechanism for identification for the audience is also the predication model: the referent is identified as a thing which the description fits. A problem, however, lies in the mechanism for introducing a thing into discourse *qua* particular by specific reference. This cannot be produced by the predication model, since the latter introduces a thing *qua* member of a kind. And it cannot be produced on the figure-ground model, since that would result in an identification of the referent *qua* particular for the audience, which is absent from specific reference. Reconsider examples (15) and (16A). In (15) the speaker indicates his intent to introduce the referent *qua* particular into the proposition by talk- ing about it *qua* particular in the context. The same holds for (16A). The difference between (15) and (16A) is that the speaker is able to identify the referent on his own in the situation given for (15), but not in the one given for (16A). However, in the latter situation he knows of the referent *qua* particular from other peo- ple. Thus, in both cases the speaker is connected with and depends upon someone's ability to pick out the referent *qua* particular. It looks, then, as though the mechanism underlying specific reference has two ingredients: an intent to talk about a thing *qua* particu- lar, as shown by the contents of the discourse (which may show whether the reference is rigid as in (15) and (16A), or whether the reference is general and not to any individual *qua* particular), and a connection to knowledge capable of picking out the referent *qua* particular. The latter knowledge would be perceptual, the same kind needed for indexical reference based on the physical sur- roundings, but this does not imply that anyone in fact refers to the referent by an indexical. However, one may doubt whether the pro- posed epistemic ingredient is a linguistic requirement for refer- ence, or a moral requirement for veracity. Consider an example. I say to my friend Harold who has just broken up with his woman friend:

17. A certain young woman in the M.B.A. program is bright, energetic, and attractive. She is a practical person also, and you would be happier with that kind of person.

Suppose Harold asks me who she is, and I reply that I don't know; I just figured out from the large number of women in the M.B.A. program that there must be such a woman in it. In this case, my use of (17) was deceptive; I gave the impression that I knew of a woman *qua* particular, when in fact I did not. Therefore, my reference in (17) raises problems about my veracity. However, in some sense, my reference in (17) was also defective; the context indicated that my reference by means of 'a certain young woman' aimed at enabling me to talk about a woman *qua* particular, but it did not do that. I incline toward taking (17) as showing that both the discourse context and the speaker's knowing (either on his own or through someone else) about the referent *qua* particular are needed for specific reference, but my mind is not settled on the point about knowledge.

There is no universal morpho-syntactic marker in English for the specific *vs.* non-specific distinction. On occasion the word 'certain' may mark specific reference, but this marker is neither a necessary nor a sufficient condition for such reference. It may be present when the RE is used to make non-specific reference, for example:

18. All poor teachers pick a certain student in each class to be their favorite.

Note that (18) is just a variant of (6) in which it was shown that 'a specific F' could be used to make non-specific reference. The possibility of using 'a certain F' or 'a specific F' to make non-specific reference derives from the status of 'certain' and 'specific' as adjectives which can be quantified over: this is what is done in (6) and (18), so that the indefinite REs in each are quantified rather than singular. The existential quantifier captures the point of introducing a thing *qua* member of a kind, as contrasted to doing so *qua* particular. However, simple existential quantification over 'a certain student' in (18) would allow *one or more* students to be favorites of each teacher, whereas (18) clearly indicates reference to a *single* student in relation to each teacher. Therefore, a predicate logic representation of (18) needs something beyond simple existential quantification in order to limit the reference of 'a certain student' to a single person in relation to each teacher.

Because there is no universal syntactic marker for the specific *vs.* non-specific distinction, one must look instead at the semantic content of indefinite REs to see whether they introduce a thing *qua* particular or *qua* member of a kind. *Qua* particular introduction results in singular non-quantified reference, whereas *qua* member of a kind introduction results in a general or quantified proposition, and these differences have effects on negation and rigidity which can be used as tests for underlying differences in manners of reference. Note that the difference between singular and quantified reference is a matter of logic, and thus quite distinct from the direct reference theory: the latter is mainly a metaphysical theory that explains singular reference by supposing that certain REs contribute the referent itself, rather than a logical complex, to propositions.

C. Support for the Present Account of the Specific-Non-specific Distinction

Most of the support for the present account of the distinction between specific and non-specific reference has been given as the account was developed. By viewing reference as constituted by two distinct actions, introducing a thing into a proposition and identifying it for the audience, there is room for determining the reference in the first of these *qua* particular, and in the second *qua* member of a kind. This account fits well with intuitions about examples in which we intend to talk about an individual *qua* particular even though we are unwilling or unable to identify it *qua* particular. The account also explains the logical features of specific reference and non-specific reference in regard to negation and rigidity of designation.

This positive support for the present accounts needs to be supplemented by comparing it to alternative accounts, which I do in the following section.

III. Polemics

Linguists have offered various theories of the nature of the distinction between specific and non-specific reference. I will discuss two of the more prominent theories that have been offered: (A) scope of quantifiers, and (B) a view developed by Barbara Hall Partee. However, before discussing these alternative views, I must first point out that the common procedure of marking the distinction by "+ [−] specific" is not a theory of the distinction but merely a notation for the distinction. If there were some general theory about what semantic markers are and how they work, and a specific theory about how the "+ [−] specific" marker in particular works, then such markers would provide some sort of theory of the distinction. However, there are no such theories.

A. Scope Distinctions

In reaction to the "+ [−] specific" marking of the distinction, several linguists opt for an account of the distinction by means of scope of quantifiers (e.g., Bach (1968), MacCawley (1970), and Kartunnen (1971)). W. V. Quine (1956 in 1971: 102) also takes scope to explicate this distinction, though he does not call it the 'specific-non-specific' distinction. In this view, 'a fish' in (19) would be analyzed as making specific reference in (19 A), and as making non-specific reference in (19 B):

19.   John wants to catch a fish.

19 A.   There is an x such that x is a fish and John wants to catch x.

19 B.   John wants there to be an x such that x is a fish and John catches x.

Numerous objections have been raised against the scope interpretation of the specific *vs.* non-specific distinction. The simplest objection to this analysis is that cases exist in which non-specific reference occurs despite the fact that there is no place to vary scope so as to assign narrow scope to the RE;[12] in other words, only wide scope for the quantifier is possible, for example:

20. A child is crying. I wonder which one it is?

Suppose that (20) is said by a mother to her husband when she hears crying coming from the room in which their two children are sleeping; the mother does not know which child is crying, and says (20). In (20) 'a child' introduces a thing into a proposition as a member of a kind and not as a particular. The negation of (20) would have to be a general rather than a singular proposition, thus showing that (20) was a quantified rather than a singular proposition.

A second very simple objection to the scope interpretation of specific-non-specific distinction concerns a logical howler, which seems not to have been noticed, in taking the wide scope of an existential quantifier to handle specific reference as in (19 A). To say that there is an x such that x is a fish and John wants to catch x states (or implies) via the English word 'an' (etymologically related to 'one') that there is *one* fish involved, but the existential quantifier involves no such statement or implication that one fish is involved. Rather, the existential quantifier produces a statement that a set is non-empty; but the non-empty set may have one or more members, and the existential quantifier is neutral between these alternatives. Thus, the specific reading of (19) is not equivalent to a wide scope existentially quantified sentence like (19 A) because the latter fails to represent the point that a single fish is the object of John's wants on the specific reading. A related logical problem is present in the non-specific interpretation. The existential quantifier in (19 B) produces reference to one or more fish, and not to *a* fish. What (19 B) translates is not (19), but

19'. John wants to catch (existing) fish.

If a predicationally modeled RE is to determine a set with only one member, an attributively used *definite* description must be used, rather than an existentially quantified description, for example:

21. The winner of last week's lottery has not claimed it yet.

22. If the weighted ping pong balls had been used in last week's lottery, the winner of last week's lottery would have been different.

Suppose that the initial RE of (21) is handled by existential quantification over a set that has only one member in it: such quantification would not provide *specific* reference, as shown by the non-rigidity of the same RE in (22) used in the same circumstances.

The third problem in the attempt to use wide scope to explain specific reference concerns rigidity and non-rigidity of designation, for example:

23. If John had wanted to catch a certain fish, he would have gone to Maine because that is the home state of that fish.

If the specific reference made in (23) by 'a certain fish' is represented by quantification, then it can pick out different referents in relation to different possible circumstances, whereas it should be a rigid designator of the same individual fish. Placing the existential quantifier outside of the 'if'-clause would solve this problem, but would produce new problems. Many philosophers would object to this procedure because it requires quantifying into a counter-factual context, but I do not wish to get into this issue. Giving wide scope to the existential quantifier also shares in the problem mentioned earlier of failing to distinguish referring to one fish from referring to one or more fish. And finally, the wide scope for the existential quantifier over 'fish' requires that the speaker make an existential claim about the fish, which (23) in no way requires of him, since he might know, and John might not know, that the fish in question was caught and eaten a year ago.

B. Partee's Account

Barbara Hall Partee refers to the specific-non-specific distinction as the referential-attributive distinction, because she believes that the two distinctions are identical. Her account of the distinction is as follows:

> The prominence of one or the other reading appears to depend on the relation between the significance of the description used in the noun phrases and whatever else is asserted in the sentence. The italicized noun phrases in the following sentences are most likely to be interpreted referentially, since their descriptive content has no particularly strong relation to the content of the rest of the sentence, and is much more easily interpretable as intended to identify or partially identify a particular individual. (1970: 362–363)

The contrast Partee cites here as basic to the distinction concerns whether the descriptive content has a relation to the rest of the context (for non-specific reference), or does not have such a relation (for specific reference). She also says that in the latter case, the descriptive content serves to identify or partially identify a particular individual, but this point fails to clarify the distinction because particular individuals are also partially identified in non-specific reference. We are then left with the point that in non-specific reference, a strong semantic relation exists between the indefinite RE and the rest of the sentence. Partee develops this notion with the help of examples. She says that in non-specific reference "the concern is not with naming a particular object but with giving descriptive characteristics which are semantically significant as part of the content of the sentence" (1970: 363); as an example she gives:

24. Since I heard that from a doctor, I am inclined to take it seriously.

She says that in this sentence we may suppose that whatever it was that the speaker heard was something to which the special competence of doctors is relevant. Because of the strong semantic relation between 'a doctor' and the rest of the sentence, Partee takes 'a doctor' in this context to make non-specific reference. I take it that Partee's notion of a strong semantic relation between an indefinite RE and the rest of a sentence makes the point that the subject of the propositional attitude has a strong interest in the kind associated with the description in the indefinite RE, because this is what occurs in (24). If this is not an appropriate interpretation of the 'strong relation,' then I do not know what to make of it.

Though Partee's notion of a strong semantic relation between an RE and the rest of the sentence has some value for picking out non-specific reference, it has a number of problems. First, note that it is at most a *criterion* for the distinction rather than an *explanation* of the nature of the distinction. This is shown by two points: first, it characterizes only one of the two members of the distinction; and second, this characterization of non-specific reference does not analyze such reference or explain why non-specific reference produces the strong semantic relation. However, even as a criterion of the distinction, a strong semantic relation between the descriptive content and the rest of the sentence fails for three reasons.

First, Partee's criterion is imprecise: how strong is a strong semantic relation? In addition, the criterion of a strong semantic relation between an RE and the rest of the sentence applies only to indefinite REs in contexts of propositional attitude, because the strong relation is between the beliefs of the subject of the attitude and the kind described by the indefinite RE. Since, as Partee notes, the specific-non-specific distinction is not limited to attitudinal contexts, her criterion is inadequate. Finally, the criterion is neither a necessary nor a sufficient condition for non-specific reference in attitudinal contexts. Consider the following examples:

25. Since I heard that from a certain doctor whom I have known for twenty years and think very highly of, I'm inclined to take it seriously. If she were wrong about this diagnosis, I would be surprised.

26. If you would give Johnnie a certain apple from that tree, he would be very happy because it is the biggest apple that he has ever seen.

In (25) the reference is specific, as shown by the use of 'certain' without quantification over it, and yet (25) is parallel to (24) and has the same strong semantic relation between the indefinite RE and the rest of the sentence. In (26), there is a strong semantic relation between the indefinite RE 'a certain apple' and the rest of the sentence (he would be happy because it is the biggest apple he has seen) but the indefinite RE makes specific reference, as shown by the rigidity of 'a certain apple from that tree.' Since these examples contain indefinite REs which make specific reference despite the strong semantic relations between the REs and the rest of the sentences, such relations are not a sufficient condition for non-specific reference.

Nor is a strong semantic relation between an indefinite RE and the rest of the sentence a necessary condition for non-specific reference. Consider the following three examples:

27 A.   Jane wants to marry a man who is rich. She does not know any rich men, but she has always wanted to be rich.

27 B.   Jane wants to marry a man who is rich. However, she does not know that he is rich.

27 C.   Jane wants to marry a man who is rich. Tom, Dick, and Harry are the men that she loves; they are all rich, though she does not know it, and she would like to marry any one of them.

Since the sentence containing 'a man who is rich' is the same in all three examples, the checking of the semantic relation to the rest of the sentence is not a simple matter. One must first interpret the sentence on the basis of its semantic relation to the surrounding discourse, and then see if the indefinite description has a strong semantic connection to the rest of the sentence as so interpreted. In the case of (27 A), the reference to 'a man who is rich' is intuitively non-specific because no particular individual is involved, and it is also non-specific on Partee's criterion because there is a strong semantic connection between the wants of the subject of the attitude and richness. In contrast, in (27 B), the reference to 'a man who is rich' is intuitively specific; this could be shown by the fact that the following singular negation would be appropriate to (27 B), but not to (27 A):

28. No, he is not rich.

According to Partee's criterion, the reference in (27 B) also seems specific because there is no semantic connection between Jane's wants and richness. However, in (27 C), the reference is intuitively non-specific because it is not to a particular thing, but rather to someone or other of a group of three. However, on Partee's criterion, the reference in this case appears specific, because again there is no strong semantic connection between Jane's wants and richness: she is not said to want to marry someone on the grounds of his richness, because "who is rich" in (27 C) is a non-restrictive relative clause, by means of which the speaker (and not Jane) provides added information about the referent. Therefore, this clause does not report the aspect under which the subject of the attitude wants something. I conclude that Partee's criterion for non-specific reference fails for (27 C), because the subject wants to marry someone or other of three people (thus non-specific reference is present), but there is no strong connection between the wants of the subject of the attitude and richness.

My account of the distinction between specific and non-specific reference can explain both why Partee's criterion works in cases like (27 A), and why it fails for cases like (27 C), (25), and (26). What Partee's criterion catches is that often when a thing is introduced into a proposition *qua* member of a kind, the subject of the attitude is reported to have an interest in the thing insofar as it is a member of that kind, as in (27 A). Such an interest produces a strong semantic relation between the content of the description and the rest of the sentence. However, introduction *qua* member of a kind does not require an interest by the subject of the attitude in the descriptive content of the RE, as shown by (27 C). Additionally, when a thing is introduced into a proposition *qua* particular, the subject of the propositional attitude is often reported to have an interest only in the individual *qua* particular, and not *qua* member of the kind described, as in (27 B). However, introduction *qua* particular does not rule out the possibility of reporting that the subject of the attitude is interested in both the individual and the kind which it is described as belonging to; this occurs in both (25) and (26). Therefore, Partee's criterion for distinguishing specific from non-specific reference is inadequate, and whatever success it does have can be explained by the fact that introduction of a thing into a proposition *qua* member of a kind often overlaps with a strong interest by the speaker in the kind.

IV. Summary and Prospects

The specific-non-specific distinction for indefinite descriptions has been drawn here at the cost of a further complication of the theory of reference. But the complication is of the highest importance because it provides an insight into the basic nature of reference: reference is not just one thing; rather it involves (at least) two distinct activities, introducing a thing into a proposition and identifying it for the audience. The distinction between introduction into a proposition and identification for the audience is not only explanatory, but it is also naturalistic in at least two ways. First, it provides a basis for explaining an ambiguity empirically well documented in the linguistics literature between specific and non-specific reference, and second, the new ingredients in the account (introduction into a proposition and identification for the audience) are fairly close to obvious uses to which we put reference: we use reference to talk about things, and to let the audience know what we are talking about. However, the notion of introduction into a proposition raises serious difficulties. In the next chapter, these difficulties are discussed and used to motivate a pair of hypotheses to replace the notion of introduction into a proposition.

Chapter 6

Attention-Directing Models for the Basic Nature
of Reference

I. Introduction

The functions of introducing a thing into a proposition and identifying it for the audience do not concern the manner or means of determining reference, but rather the *uses* or *purposes* to which the determination of reference is put. Since the purposes of an activity indicate its fundamental nature, it appears that reference is constituted by two rather different functions: one function relates reference to the audience, and the other to the rest of discourse.

Although the functions of introducing a thing into a proposition and identifying it for the audience are useful for an intuitive understanding of the basic nature of reference, the first of these needs further clarification and development. This is because the notion of introducing a thing into a proposition is metaphorical, and seems to bring with it the direct reference theory. I will develop a non-metaphorical replacement for the notion of 'introducing a thing into a proposition,' and show how it avoids the direct reference theory.

II. A Non-metaphorical Replacement for Introduction of a Thing Into a Proposition

We know what it is to introduce one person to another, or to introduce bacteria into a nutrient medium, but what is it to introduce a thing into a proposition? In fact, 'introduction into a proposition' is a metaphorical way of treating the usual means by which an individual is made available for being talked about. But how do we describe this means non-metaphorically? A clue to answering this question is found in the resemblance of introduction into a proposition to identification for the audience: both of these functions involve a determination of the referent. However, each determination has a different purpose: identification for hearers aims at informing them of which thing or what kind of thing is the referent, whereas introduction into a proposition aims at contributing to the content of the discourse. The latter purpose requires relating an output from the determination of reference to other things in discourse. These other things in discourse are also objects of attention directing. This means that introduction into a proposition includes two factors, specification of the referent, and a relating of an output from that specification to other objects of attention directing. We can now state in a non-metaphorical way the three basic functions which constitute reference:

(a) *Specificatory function*: directing attention (of both speaker and hearer) to a thing for purposes of relating an output from this function to other things in discourse

(b) *Relating function*: directing attention (of both speaker and hearer) to the output from the specificatory function as related to other objects of attention directing

(c) *Identificatory (for audience) function*: directing the attention of the hearers to the referent so that they can identify it.

Since these three basic functions of reference and the various models for determining reference are all varieties of attention directing, I call my account of reference 'the attention directing view' of reference. This view comprises a family of models of various levels of generality.

How can one thing, like reference, have more than one function? Consider a parallel. A fork has the function of conveying food to the mouth, and the additional function of grasping food by means of spearing it; the latter function is not present in a spoon. Not only does a fork have two functions, but their relationship parallels that of the specificatory and relating functions. Just as a fork is used to spear food in order to convey it to the mouth, so also the specificatory function is used to determine a referent in order to relate it to other objects of attention directing.

The specificatory and relating functions are non-metaphorical replacements for the notion of introduction into a proposition. The identificatory (for audience) function is the same as in the last chapter. Although the three functions are described here in a very general way, more specific varieties of them are always present in reference. For instance, the attention directing in the specificatory and identificatory functions requires some particular mechanism (e.g., the figure-ground or predication models) and manner of reference (e.g., *qua* particular or *qua* member of a kind). The description of the relating function is also extremely general in that it does not specify either the output from (a) the specificatory function or from the other objects of attention directing. The output from (a) is attention directing to a thing, and it includes two aspects, the attention directing itself, and its focus on a certain object (or kind of object). I believe that both aspects are always present in (a), but that the relating function may relate one or both of them to other objects of attention directing.

Which of the alternative outputs from the specificatory function is picked up by the relating function depends on the other factors in discourse, that is, the other ingredients, besides reference, in various kinds of contexts. We must understand these contexts or settings in order to understand how the outputs from the specificatory function are related to these other things. Among the settings for reference are a wide variety of propositions, for example, subject-predicate, existence, identity, and propositional attitudes. I view subject-predicate propositions as constituted by the attention directing of reference as related to the attention directing of predication, plus a speech act. I view speech acts not as attention directing, but as stances taken toward certain kinds of complexes of attention directing. Obviously, I cannot develop full explanatory models for predication, propositions, and speech acts here; I have more than enough work to do on reference.[1] Nevertheless, the different kinds of propositions named above have certain features that interact with reference in interesting ways. Besides the propositional settings for reference, there are also non-propositional ones, for example, within interjections and vocatives. These various settings determine what the relating function selects from the specificatory function. The most common setting for the relating function of reference is within propositions, but I postpone discussing this setting until the next chapter. Here I discuss two kinds of non-propositional settings for the relating function, interjections and vocatives.[2]

REs play roles in interjections; consider an example:

1. That idiot! I should never have taken this job!

The speaker uses the initial RE of (1) to direct attention to a certain person *qua* particular, but he does not assert anything of him. Instead, attention is directed to him *qua* particular as related to a certain affective state expressed by the speaker. Thus, this use of the RE 'That idiot' both specifies a referent and relates it to other objects of attention directing[3] (namely, the speaker's attitude and feelings).

Besides being related to things within propositions or within interjections, the referent *qua* specified may also be related to a piece of discourse as a whole, in that attention is directed to the referent as the one to whom the discourse is addressed, for example:

2. Obedience to authority is what makes the army what it is. Hey, four-eyes in the first row! Without respect for authority, organization would be impossible.

Suppose that (2) is an excerpt from a drill sergeant's lecture to new recruits. He added the phrase, 'Hey, four-eyes in the first row' because he noticed a certain recruit gazing off into the distance. The use of this RE directs attention to a certain recruit, not in order to assert or talk about his possession of certain properties or relations, but rather to bring to his attention that he is a subject to whom discourse is being addressed. Thus, the relating function relates him to the discourse as a whole. This contrasts to relating the output from the specificatory function to what is expressed by parts of the discourse, as is the case in the relations to factors within propositions and within interjections.

In allowing the output from the specificatory function to be related to non-propositional objects of attention directing, the present theory departs from the commonly accepted Fregean view that reference occurs only in a sentence. Reference within interjections and reference by vocatives are both extra-sentential. However, I retain a more general version of the Fregean insight: reference is not merely a matter of designating a thing, but always involves an additional function that relates the referent to other things in discourse. Discourse, however, includes non-propositional factors.

Arguments for the Threefold Basic Functioning of Reference

My main argument for the threefold functioning of reference is the same as the one developed in the previous chapter: if reference is constituted by the three types of attention-directing involved in the specificatory, relating, and identificatory (for audience) functions, then we can make sense of the distinction between specific and non-specific reference made by means of indefinite descriptions. In the specific use, a description identifies a thing for the audience *qua* member of a kind, but specifies it *qua* particular so as to relate an output to other objects of attention directing. In the non-specific use, however, a description not only identifies a thing for the audience *qua* member of a kind, but also specifies it *qua* member of a kind for the purpose of relating it *qua* specified to other things in discourse. The presence of specification *qua* particular or *qua* member of a kind is shown by the discourse context (usually more than one sentence is required). In contexts in which an indefinite description is used to specify a referent, it is usually clear whether the referent is being related *qua* particular or *qua* member of a kind to a predicate because of the different results each would have under negation or in counter-factual contexts.

Additional support for the attention directing models can be found by comparing them to the direct reference theory. The replacement of the notion of 'introducing a thing into a proposition' by the specificatory and relating functions removes any suggestion of the direct reference theory, because only attention-directing, and not actual physical objects, are ingredients in propositions. This uniform account of propositions avoids the metaphysical anomaly of having an actual physical object mixed up with logical complexes so as to constitute a proposition.[4] Some advocates of the direct reference theory avoid such mixtures by using properties and relations in propositions to replace logical complexes.[5] Though this move makes for a more consistent metaphysics, the resultant theories seem unconnected to natural language. At most, such theories might specify meanings and referents, but they offer no explanation of how referents are connected with language.

Not only do the attention-directing models provide uniform constituents for propositions, but they are not other-worldly entities like possible worlds (construed non-linguistically). Although attention-directings are abstract entities, they clearly exist: people do direct attention to things, *qua* particular and *qua* member of a kind, and as related to other things to which attention is also directed, and in order to identify things for hearers. Attention-directings are naturalistic social-psychological entities. Most importantly, the attention-directing theory provides fairly clear models for connecting these social-psychological entities with relatively concrete entities (words, gestures, and contexts).

Additional support for the distinction between the specificatory and relating functions can be found in morpho-syntactic features of REs. Case (in inflected languages) plus word order indicate the relationship between what a use of an RE expresses and the other objects of attention-directing in discourse. In contrast to this marking of relations by case and word order, the stems of words, as well the speaker's actions and gestures in the context, mark the specification of the referent. Since such different means are used to mark the specificatory and relating functions in reference, one may reasonably conclude that these are distinct functions within reference.[6]

Empirical studies in linguistics provide a reason for distinguishing the identification of the referent for the audience from relating the referent to other objects of attention-directing. Linguists speak of left-dislocation as "a transformation that moves an RE out of and to the left of a clause, leaving in its place a coreferential pronoun" (Ochs and Schieffelin (1983: 143) who attribute this definition to Ross (1967)), for example:

3. Uh Pat McGee. I don't know if you know him, he—he lives in Palisades.

4. And my father, oh he's, he's fit to be tied.[7]

The linguists cite examples like these in unplanned discourse, as contrasted to planned or written discourse. I view left dislocation as separating the function of identifying the referent for the audience from that of relating the referent to other objects of attention-directing.[8] Also, the speaker may check up on whether this initial identificatory information suffices for the hearer or not, and if it does not, he may give more identificatory information before stating the proposition that he wishes to communicate.[9] This separating of the identificatory (for the audience) and relating functions gives reason to believe that these are distinct functions generally, even when they are not separated. I conclude that the basic tripartite model for reference is supported not only by the semantics of the specific-non-specific distinction but also by considerations of metaphysics and of empirical linguistics.

The attention-directing family of models for reference is complex, especially when compared to extensional views of reference, or the direct reference theory. However, the complexity of the present theory is not objectionable on grounds of explanatory economy, unless one can find simpler accounts of the same facts of communication and logical intuitions. Nor is the complexity of the attention-directing view of reference objectionable on ontological grounds, as was argued above.

III. The Role of Extensions in the Theory of Reference

Reference in current philosophy is often treated as extensional, that is, reference is taken to be nothing but pairing off things (whether in actual or possible worlds) with REs.[10] This view yields necessary and sufficient conditions for reference; an RE refers just in case it has a referent. Such an extensional treatment, however, uses a *result* of reference (having an extension) without treating the mechanisms of reference. Moreover, the emphasis within extensional theories is on the results of extensions of REs for truth conditions. Extensional views thus focus on results that are *two steps removed from the mechanisms* of reference, and this leads to neglect of the basic nature of reference, the diverse manners and means of determining reference, and the role of REs in interjections and vocatives. Treating reference extensionally also leads to recurring problems about reference in certain contexts, to be discussed in the next chapter.

On the attention-directing view of reference, having an extension is a *result* of the activity of referring, rather than an essential ingredient in that activity. The achievement of this result is usually a major goal of acts of reference, but not the only goal. Given the speaker's intention of specifying a thing for purposes of talking about it, he must also have the goal of using appropriate means (RE, actions, and gestures) for conveying that reference in the context. Yet another goal is that of having the hearer discern the reference. These goals of using appropriate means for referring, and having the audience discern the reference, are distinct from that of having a real referent for the RE as it is used. This last goal, which is the essential one for extensional treatments of reference, need not always be present, as we will see in the next chapter.

The distinction that I am drawing between an activity and its goals is a traditional one. Aristotle (*Nicomachaean Ethics*, bk. I) held that some activities, for example, contemplation, have no goal beyond themselves, but many things we do are goal-directed, for example, building a bridge so that one has a means of crossing a river, or running a race in order that one might win. I view reference as an activity of directing attention in a certain way in a context, which is aimed (usually) at the goal of creating a connection with a real thing so that one can talk about it. An RE's connection with a real thing is its having a referent (or an extension), and is not an activity, like running a race, but rather the achievement of a goal of the activity, like winning a race.[11] Therefore, on the attention-directing view of reference, having a referent is not a necessary condition for reference.

The lack of a necessary connection between reference and a referent raises at least two difficulties:

(a) How can communication work satisfactorily if REs only *usually* have a referent?

(b) How can the importance of extensions be explained if they are not essential to reference?

(a) My answer to the problem of only usually having a referent is that any looseness of correlation between a use of an RE and a referent is orderly rather than haphazard, and essential if reference is to do the empirical work required of it. The empirical basis for reference lies in human experience and beliefs, both of which are fallible. Therefore, reference must involve a fallible connection between a use of an RE and a referent. This connection is nevertheless orderly because uses of REs are connected to referents on the basis of mechanisms like those of the figure-ground and predication models. These models as applied to the context determine whether or not there is a referent. Since the hearers of uses of REs act in accord with these models, they can discern the presence or absence of a referent.

(b) Even though extensions are not essential to acts of reference on the attention-directing view, they are important because of our purposes in referring, and because of the way we learn the skill of referring. The main reason why we refer to things is to enable us to talk about them. This purpose is especially clear in relation to things that affect our survival or happiness. Referring would be useful for such purposes only if it usually or at least often did enable us to talk about things that really exist. But an automatic and infallible connection between REs and things is not available to us humans, because we refer on the basis of fallible beliefs.

Learning how to refer and to understand acts of reference requires the existence of a referent, if the attention-directing view of reference is correct. The essential ingredient in making reference to something is the directing of attention to it according to certain conventions. In order to *learn* these conventions, that is, to learn how to understand uses of REs, and how to use them oneself, one must play language games involving REs and real objects to which the REs direct attention. If the first language game one played involved REs which had no referents, one would not grasp the language game of making reference. However, once we have mastered the language games of referring by playing them in situations with real referents, we can engage in the attention-directing techniques of such games even in the absence of appropriate objects of reference.

The view of reference developed here has no need for intentional entities as objects of reference. The use of an RE directs attention to a thing on the basis of the figure-ground, predication, or other model. If we know how to refer, we can use REs to direct attention to things which do not exist. To hold that in such cases the RE refers to an intentional entity raises large problems: either what goes on in the act of reference is quite different in cases involving existing and nonexisting referents, and this difference needs an account, or reference is the same in each case, namely, reference to an intentional object. But on the latter alternative, an account is needed not only of the nature of intentional objects, but also of their relations to real entities. My preference is to avoid these problems by holding that what uniformly occurs in reference, whether or not a real entity is the referent, are certain types of attention-directing (on the figure-ground, predication, or other models). One variety of success for such attention-directing is that there exists an appropriate object for the attention-directing. But the attention-directing can be understood, once the basic language games of reference are mastered, whether or not such success is present.

IV. Summary and Prospects

In chapters II through VI, a major focus has been the explanatory power of the models for reference in regard to communication and logical intuitions. In regard to the latter, the models explain rigidity of designation and certain features of negation. In regard to communication, they account for several features. For indexicals, they explain the importance of perception and of the context in discerning the referent, and the communication of which thing is the referent. For definite descriptions, the models explain the referential-attributive distinction, assimilating referentially used definite descriptions to indexicals. This also explains how definite descriptions with little content (e.g., 'the dog') determine a unique referent. For indefinite descriptions, the models explain the specific-non-specific distinction, and the connection of specific reference by means of indefinite descriptions with common human purposes in reference.

The present hypotheses for reference can be developed and

supported in various directions. One is to apply the hypotheses to traditional problems about reference, for example, reference to the nonexistent, the informativeness of identity statements, and the problems of referential opacity and transparency. Such applications will clarify some implications of the hypotheses, and will support them by showing their explanatory power. This will be done in the next chapter.

Chapter 7

Applications of the Models to Existence and Identity Contexts and to Opacity

Introduction

The strongest support for an explanatory hypothesis is its fruitfulness in dealing with phenomena beyond those which prompted its creation. In this chapter, I try to provide such support for the attention-directing models by applying them to traditional problems about reference in certain problematical contexts, including existence and identity statements, and contexts of propositional attitude. These puzzles concerning reference first appeared, along with the predicate-logic paradigm, in Gottlob Frege's work. Their difficulty stems from their combination of reference, which is not well understood, with certain types of context that are also not well understood. The predicate-logic paradigm, in my opinion, heightens these problems into paradoxes. I view them as genuine problems but pseudo-paradoxes; the latter disappear when the problems are viewed from the perspective of the attention-directing models for reference. These models also lead to the beginnings of solutions to the problems. But since the problematical contexts are part of the problem, explanatory models are needed for them also.

In response to the problems about referential opacity and about identity contexts, a large literature has developed. I will not make much use of this literature because my accounts are developed from a different perspective, that of my theory of reference; also, limitations of space make it impossible to include a survey of the literature.

I. Existence and Identity Contexts

In the early days of the predicate-logic tradition, paradoxes appeared concerning existence and identity contexts, and Russell and Frege offered ways to deal with them. Russell took the meaning of genuine REs to be nothing but their extensions. But if such an RE is the subject term in an 'existence claim' (I use 'existence claim' for claims of existence or of nonexistence), the claim is either meaningless or trivial. If such an RE lacks an extension, then the claim is meaningless, and if it has an extension, then a positive existence claim is trivially true, and a negative existence claim is contradictory.

Russell handled the paradox by treating most REs of natural language not as genuine referring expressions, but rather as descriptions (including disguised descriptions) which function in virtue of being true of their referents. In this model, most existence claims are used to assert that a certain description is satisfied. The only examples of genuine referring expressions, according to Russell (1914 in 1956; 1918 in 1956: 201), were 'this' and 'that' (sometimes he included 'I'). These, according to Russell, require immediate acquaintance with their referents, so that the referent itself is in the proposition. Thus, Russell accepts the paradox that existence claims are either meaningless or trivial when genuine REs are involved. Nor does he reject the paradox for REs which are interpreted as descriptions; instead he sidesteps it by holding that they are not genuine REs.

Identity contexts resemble existence contexts in causing problems and paradoxes within the predicate-logic tradition. The problem for identity claims concerns how they can be informative, and the paradox is that a mere understanding of an identity claim is sufficient for knowing its truth or falsity. The paradox arises when REs function non-predicatively in an identity claim because then one must discern their referents in order to understand the REs. However, if one discerns their referents, one thereby discerns the truth or falsity of the identity claim. Whereas if one does not discern the referents of the REs in an identity claim, one does not understand the claim. Therefore, it seems that identity claims (whose REs function non-predicatively) cannot be informative, since merely to understand them, one must already know all that is needed to discern their truth value. Although the traditional paradoxes for identity and existence statements are parallel, they differ in that the one for identity claims concerns epistemic features (being either non-understandable, or obviously true or obviously false), whereas the one for existence claims concerns logical features (being either meaningless, or tautological or contradictory).

Frege's solution to the paradox for identity claims was to distinguish sense and reference.[1] Senses are ways of presenting the referent. Because one grasps referents through senses, one may know the same referent under two different ways of presenting it, without knowing that these different senses present the same referent. Identity statements inform a person that two different senses present the same referent.

Both this Fregean view of identity contexts, and his theory of senses, have been rejected by many philosophers within the predicate-logic tradition. Without senses, it is still easy to analyze identity statements containing predicative REs into claims that two different predicates are satisfied by the same individual. But if the REs cannot be reduced to predicates, paradoxes arise, at least if reference is treated extensionally. I define extensionality of reference as follows: the extension of an RE, and only its extension, affects the semantics of statements containing it.[2] These paradoxes arise for both identity and existence claims. If you place the extension of an RE into the semantic analysis of an existence statement, you make that statement either trivially true or contradictory. (If the RE had no extension, then the analysis would have a gap, and be meaningless.) Similarly, if you place the extensions of REs into the semantic analyses of identity statements, one need only look at those extensions to see if the claim is true or false.[3]

Can these paradoxes by avoided? Yes. The motivation for treating reference extensionally is both a priori and top-down, based on a desire for the simplicity provided by a system of extensional logic. If one takes a naturalistic approach to the study of reference, one would prefer an approach which is empirical, and includes both bottom-up and top-down reasoning. Such an approach is found in the basic tripartite model for reference, and in the figure-ground model. But even if we already have a viable account of reference, how are we to treat existence and identity contexts? We can try to find out something about their functioning by looking at their purposes. I do this from two directions: from their use in communication, and from the attention-directing model for reference. The latter direction might seem circular, but it is not, because the arguments for the models did not depend on existence and identity contexts.

According to the attention-directing model, speakers direct attention to referents on the basis of their knowledge of the referents and of contexts containing them. But this knowledge of things in the world and of contexts is empirical; we have no automatic or a priori access to referents. Because of the way we gain knowledge of referents, we can make mistakes about them, so that our referential devices need correction and development.

Many processes of correcting and developing beliefs are carried on with the help of language. Are the beliefs underlying our referential apparatus also capable of being worked on and improved with the help of language? Of course. Consider some examples. Suppose a drunk is having *delerium tremens*, and says,

1. "That pink elephant is coming toward us."

The bartender replies to the drunk

2. "That pink elephant does not exist."

The claim of nonexistence in (2) prunes the drunk's referential apparatus: it rejects a way of specifying reference *qua* particular which fails by a wide margin to specify a referent in the real world. Such pruning is important to humans because reference concerns the interface of language and the world; removing a referential device because it lacks a referent, affects one's expectations and behavior, for example, the drunk does not have to take actions to avoid being trampled by a mere elephant-hallucination.

If an RE fails to have a referent by a narrow margin, a claim of identity that links the attention-directing of a use of one RE with different attention-directing via another RE would be a useful correction. Suppose that a woman says (with some gesture) to a friend,

3. "That man over there in a tweed coat is my cousin."

Her friend replies,

4. "There is no man over there in a tweed coat."

This is a claim of nonexistence, which says that a certain referential device fails to specify anything in the real world. The first speaker replies,

5. "He is that person with the hair sticking straight up."

Because the description in (3) did not work well as a figure, the first speaker uses (5), an identity statement, which connects a new figure with her first reference. This is an addition to the referential apparatus, aimed at improving its accuracy, and thereby improving communication.

If the attention-directing of reference is adequate, but nevertheless is missed by the hearer, an identity claim is also useful to help the hearer make the referential connection, for example:

6. "That Gothic building is my old high school."

Suppose that the hearer of (6) asks 'which one do you mean?,' and the speaker replies (while pointing),

7. "It is that building to the left of the movie theatre."

This identity statement gives the hearer a new way of picking out the same referent. The speaker adds to his referential devices because, although the first device was correct, it did not work in communication.

In the situation given for (6) and (7), the hearer was able to use one referential device but not the other to pick out the referent. There are also cases in which a hearer can use each of two different devices to pick out a referent, but fails to know that each device picks out the same particular individual. For instance, suppose that a man sees the back of a person's head in a mirror, and comments on the funny haircut of that person. His companion replies,

8. "That man whose head is reflected in the mirror over there is you."

In this case, two different referential devices are consolidated so that both are taken to direct attention to a certain single person.[4] This information was previously unknown to the hearer, even though he already knew the reference of both of the main REs in (8). The mere fact that we can grasp reference to a thing on one basis has no implications at all for our ability to grasp it on some other basis. We often need to be told, as in (8), that different ways of specifying reference specify a certain individual. Claims of nonidentity have the reverse function, and are used when two ways of specifying reference, which had been thought to specify the same thing, are found not to do so.

Examples like (1) through (8) above lead me to believe that the whole point of existence and identity contexts is to improve the referential apparatus by removing mistakes, or giving additional information about reference, including the information that two different ways of specifying reference specify the same thing. Similar views, at least regarding the purpose of identity statements, have been held by Gottlob Frege (1879), Peter F. Strawson (1950 in 1963: 190–192; 1974), Michael Lockwood (1971), John T. Kearns (1984), and Thomas V. Morris (1984). I differ from most of these philosophers, however, in that I assign *propositional* status in an identity statement to the mechanisms for improving the referential apparatus.[5]

On the basis of this account of the purposes of existence and identity statements, I will devise some rough models for them, which focus mainly on the contributions of indexical REs to such contexts. Both existence and identity claims comment on aspects of reference that involve its connection with the real world. Whether that connection is successful is the concern of existence contexts. Whether two ways of specifying a referent specify the same referent is the concern of identity contexts. Therefore, the ingredients in models for existence and identity statements must include ways of specifying reference, and must comment on how these relate to the real world.[6]

Indexical reference is constituted by three types of attention-directing: the specificatory and identificatory functions direct attention to a thing on the figure-ground model, and the relating function relates the attention-directing of the specificatory function to other objects of attention-directing. The specificatory function always expresses both a way of directing attention to a thing and an object of that attention-directing. This object of attention-directing need not really exist. Existence and identity contexts differ from subject-predicate contexts only in regard to the relating function. In subject-predicate statements, the relating function takes the focus on the object from the specificatory function and relates it to other objects of attention-directing. In contrast, in existence and identity claims the relating function connects the way of specifying reference, rather than a focus on the object of the specificatory attention-directing, to other objects of attention-directing. These other objects, in existence and identity claims, concern the real world, so that a comment is made about whether the way of specifying reference succeeds in specifying a thing in the real world (for existence claims) or about whether the two ways of specifying reference specify the same individual (for identity claims).

The schemas just given for existence and identity contexts leads to the following rough analyses of their ingredients. I begin with existence statements, and repeat an earlier example:

2. That pink elephant does not exist.

I symbolize a particular way of specifying reference by W plus the ingredients in the specification. The result for (2) is

2 A. W (figure: pink elephant, gesture: G_1, context: C_1) does not specify anything in the real world.

On this analysis, the speaker asserts that a certain way of specifying reference, which he uses in the subject position of the sentence, does not specify anything in the real world. A *positive* existence claim includes also an ordinary use of the subject RE to refer, for example:

9.   That pink elephant does exist.

9 A. W (figure: pink elephant, gesture: G_1, context: C_1) does specify a certain thing in the real world, namely, that pink elephant.

The last phrase is added to the analysis because a positive existence claim asserts that the way of specifying reference succeeds in specifying a real world referent; this amounts to saying that the object of the attention-directing really exists. These analyses for existence claims have two useful features. They get rid of the assumption, which made existence statements paradoxical, that an RE has a referent. Also, they are well-suited to the purpose of correcting the referential apparatus.

Are existence statements on my construal metalinguistic, that is, are they statements about expressions in a language? No, because they are about reference, which is constituted by attention-directing, which involves not only expressions, but also actions, contexts, and real-world entities. Also, metalinguistic claims are about words in particular languages, whereas existence claims are about ways of directing attention, which are social psychological entities that can be the same across different languages.

REs in identity claims are treated like those in existence claims on my models, except that identity claims usually include an assumption that the referent really exists. I repeat an earlier example:

8.   That man whose back is reflected in the mirror over there is you.

8 A. W (figure: man whose back is reflected in the mirror over there, Gesture: G_1, Context: C_1) and W (figure: addressee of the present discourse, Gesture: G_1, Context: C_1) specify you.

On this analysis, identity statements are informative because each of the W's in (8 A) is a different way of specifying a referent, so that merely being able to use each to pick out a referent does not require knowledge that they both pick out the same individual. The assumption of the existence of the referent is present in the use of 'you' at the end of (8 A).

My models for existence and identity claims include the ways of specifying reference so as to allow these claims to comment on them. But this inclusion is impossible in a semantics that fixes indexical reference by stipulations, or in direct reference semantics. Work on the referential apparatus must then be moved off to pragmatics. What's wrong with that, as long as the complete theory of language represents all that is going on within language? Nothing is wrong, if the theory is purely specificatory, and not explanatory. However, if the theory purports to represent the entities and mechanisms underlying and producing natural language, then something is wrong. In particular, if existence and identity contexts have as their basic function improving the referential apparatus, then an explanatory semantic account must reflect this.

There are several reasons to prefer the present explanatory accounts for existence and identity contexts over standard views on the topic. Its basis in the purposes of these contexts is one point in their favor, because purposes are an additional constraint on analyses, beyond truth conditions, and indicate the basic nature of things. In relation to traditional problems about existence and identity claims, the figure-ground model supplies a needed non-predicative way of specifying reference. Also, the relating function within existence and identity contexts explains how the way of specifying reference can enter into the basic semantic content of such contexts.

II. Opacity and Transparency

INTRODUCTION

The terms 'opacity' and 'transparency' are Quine's, though Frege and Russell discussed the same phenomena. Quine (1960, 1961, 1986: 290) coined the phrase 'referential opacity' to refer to contexts in which the logical principles of substitutivity or existential generalization fail.[7] He calls contexts in which these rules are valid 'referentially transparent.' Substitutivity (I use '*SUB*' for short) states that *coreferential REs can be intersubstituted salva veritate*. Existential generalization (I use '*EG*' for short) *allows one to replace an RE by an existentially quantified variable* (here is a natural language example: from 'John runs.' deduce 'There is someone who runs.'). The term 'opacity' gives the impression that something went wrong in such contexts, and Quine (1961: 143, 145, 150) reinforces this impression by saying that opacity "afflicts" contexts, and is an "infirmity" and a "root of trouble." When he first introduces the term 'opacity,' he says that REs in such contexts do not *merely* have an extension, giving the impression that they have an extension, but also do something else. However, on occasion, he (1960: 145) talks as though they do not have an extension, which is a vastly different point. The position that REs in opaque contexts have no extension also seems to follow logically from two other views held by Quine. One is the point that a quantifier outside the scope of an operator which produces an opaque context (e.g., 'it is necessary that,' 'x believes that') cannot bind variables inside the scope of that operator. The other is that reference is via bound variables. Though these two points seem to entail that reference does not occur inside opaque contexts, Quine does not draw the conclusion.[8]

Why does SUB fail in opaque contexts? One might reply that such failure is part of what we mean by 'opaque.' But this a priori answer is unsatisfying. The question I wanted to ask is this: Why does SUB fail in certain types of contexts which we call 'opaque?' This question seeks an explanation of the conditions underlying and producing the failure of SUB. Such an explanation would state what features of the contexts affect the operation of SUB, and why these features have this effect. But this explanation requires a prior explanation of the workings of SUB on REs in transparent contexts. This in turn would require explanatory accounts of the functioning of REs and of transparent contexts. Thus, answering the question of why SUB fails is complex, but the complexity is that of nested questions, which can be handled one by one. Moreover, we already have a theory of how reference works. Next we figure out why SUB works in transparent contexts (from now on, I use this as short for 'the ones we call 'transparent',' and I treat 'opaque' similarly). Then we figure out why SUB doesn't work in opaque contexts.[9]

Why does SUB hold for transparent contexts? An easy answer (too easy, in my opinion) is provided by an extensional view of reference. On this view, all that matters semantically about a use of an RE is its extension. Since coreferential REs agree on this semantic point, they make the same contribution to semantics, so that SUB would be valid.

If extensionality is not used to support SUB, how might it be supported? Some philosophers (cf. my (1985: 563, note 2)) have used the indiscernibility of identicals to support SUB, or have even identified the two principles.[10] The indiscernibility of identicals says that if two things are identical, they have all properties in common. It is puzzling why anyone would take the indiscernibility of identicals to support SUB, since the latter concerns linguistic matters (terms and sentences), which the former neither mentions nor provides implications about. Why have people thought that the indiscernibility of identicals supports SUB? Perhaps because the referent has the property of being referred to by the each of the two REs? But this concerns the relation of REs to the thing, and not the substitution of REs in sentences. The only appearance of support that I can find for SUB in the indiscernibility of identicals is found in the predicate logic formulation of the latter principle:

$$(x)\,(y)[\ (x=y) \supset (F)\,(Fx \equiv Fy)\ ]$$

The picture presented by this formula is that if 'x' and 'y' refer to the same thing, then it really doesn't matter whether one uses 'Fx' or 'Fy,' so that one could substitute the 'y' for the 'x.' Since variables in the predicate-logic paradigm are the vehicles of reference, such substitution may be viewed as standing for substituting co-referential REs. But this indicates nothing about substituting REs in natural language, since the formula above is *extensional* because it is expressed in predicate-logic, whereas natural language is not extensional (or at least it should not be settled a priori that it is extensional). In other words, the picture of support given by the formula above derives from its extensionality, and not from the indiscernibility of identicals.

Extensionality supports SUB in an a priori way, in that it is based on a feature of predicate-logic, and the support is too strong: it requires transparency always, but this does not hold for natural language, as will become clear in the discussions of particular types of opacity. To understand why SUB is often valid, we need to find *empirical and not so strong support* for it. We must ask what is there about the way people use REs to refer in natural language which makes SUB often valid. And we must not assume that our account for *SUB* will also fit *EG*, if our investigation is to be empirical.

To clarify what goes on in reference that might affect EG and SUB, I use the attention-directing model for reference, including the specificatory, relating, and identificatory functions. I begin with the use in communication of an RE as a subject within a simple subject-predicate sentence. In such use of an RE, the speaker specifies a thing so as to relate the object of the specificatory function to the relations or properties expressed by the predicate; in doing so, he usually supposes that the referent exists. This supposition arises from the fact that people's talk and their references usually concern things that really exist.[11] Because reference made by REs within simple subject-predicate statements is usually to what exists, EG is usually valid on them. This argument holds for reference in general in such contexts. A different argument can be based on the particular type of reference that uses the figure-ground model. That model requires that the referent be in the background context (or related to it by cause-effect or part-whole relations). This requires supposing that the referent really exists only if the context concerns real rather than fictional things. The physical surroundings bring in real things, but a discourse context may bring in fictional things, so that one need not suppose that referents within it really exist.[12]

The fact that the speaker usually assumes that the object of his act of referring really exists gives no reason to believe that the means for picking out the object do not matter semantically; therefore, the support just given for EG within subject-predicate contexts does not support the validity of SUB. Then why believe that SUB does hold for simple subject-predicate contexts? One reason is found in the usual *relating function* expressed by using REs in such contexts. To simplify matters, consider a sentence whose subject RE supplies a topic, and whose predicate makes a comment about that topic.[13] Whether a use of such a sentence is true depends upon whether the thing referred to by the RE has the property or relation expressed by the predicate. This means that substituting a coreferential RE will not affect the *truth value* of the use of the sentence, since that is affected by what the RE refers to, and not by the way in which the use of the RE directs attention to it. Thus, substitutivity *salva veritate* is supported by the way that the relating functions works in simple subject-predicate sentences. It should be noted, however, that this argument is limited so far to simple subject-predicate sentences, and it does not show that only the extension of RE affects the semantics of such sentences, despite its support for SUB. The conclusion that only the extension of an RE affects the semantics of sentences would be justified only if there is nothing to the semantics of a sentence except what affects its truth conditions. For this purely truth-conditional view of semantics, I have not seen any arguments except those which suggest that semantics is simpler if it is purely truth-conditional.

Another kind of context which allows SUB is a simple identity context. Does this show that REs in them function purely extensionally? No, because the validity of substitution follows from the nature of the *claim* made by identity contexts (that two ways of specifying reference specify a certain thing), which entails coreferentiality of the REs in them.[14] To conclude that such validity is produced by purely extensional functioning of REs in them would be a case of what Geach (1962: 61, 116) calls the cancelling-out fallacy. The non-extensional functioning of the REs in identity contexts is cancelled out (in relation to truth conditions) by the nature of such contexts.

The validity of the rule of EG is supported by the fact that speakers usually talk about what really exists. In contrast, the validity of SUB is supported by a point about the relating function in subject-predicate statements: the speaker relates what the specificatory function picks out to what the predicate expresses. Both cases support a statistical rather than universal basis for SUB and EG. Speakers *usually* use subject-predicate sentences with the simple relating function that supports SUB, and speakers *usually* suppose that the referents they specify exist. Are other kinds of contexts transparent? This is an empirical question. We should not generalize from the usual transparency of subject-predicate contexts to transparency in all contexts.

The origins one assigns to EG and SUB affect one's outlook on transparency and opacity. If one accepts extensionality of reference, opacity contravenes universal rules, and is paradoxical. If one rejects extensionality, and instead views EG and SUB as having the statistical bases described above, the paradox disappears. But questions still have to be answered about the causes of both transparency and opacity.

How can we reconcile the universality of EG and SUB in logic with their merely statistical applicability in natural language? One way would be to find that the statistical regularity is just a surface level phenomenon, which has universal regularity underlying it. However, the particular varieties of opacity, to be discussed shortly, do not support this; instead they show opacity as deriving from the interaction of referential mechanisms with various kinds of contexts. Another way of reconciling the universality of logical rules with the statistical regularity of natural language would be to view the former as an idealization, useful for many purposes, but not aimed at describing the basic nature of natural language.[15] Extensional logic would then be in a situation parallel to Euclidean geometry: just as the axiom of parallels is not true of real space, so also extensionality is not true of natural language. But in certain contexts one can calculate as though extensionality does hold, just as one can calculate sometimes using the axiom of parallels.

Viewing logic as an idealization of natural language differs from viewing it as providing a specificatory theory of natural language; the latter perspective assigns logic a descriptive role, though not an explanatory one. Though I view logic in general as an idealization, I think that some particular devices of logic are useful for specificatory theories that approximate natural language, and this has been borne out by the use of logic in artificial intelligence systems for natural language. However, I object to the use of logic to provide a priori descriptions or explanations of natural language.

Because the empirical support for EG and SUB differs, we might expect their range of application to differ. We will see that this does occur. In what follows, I discuss many types of opacity. My goal is to show how reference, construed according to the attention-directing models, interacts with each type of opaque context to produce the opacity.

(A) Contexts within a Quotation

Consider the example

10. 'Boston' has six letters.

Despite the fact that 'Boston' and 'The Bean Town' are coreferential, one cannot validly substitute one for the other to obtain

11. 'The Bean Town' has six letters.

A standard account of such opacity was that placing quotation marks around terms forms a new name, which names the term rather than the referent of the term. Then substitution fails because the RE substituted in (11) is not coreferential with the initial RE in (10). On this account, the principle of substitutivity is simply inapplicable (rather than false) because it applies only to coreferential REs.

John Searle (1969: 74–76) objects to the standard view on the grounds that there is no need to form a name of a word when one can simply produce the word in discourse. Searle's view can be combined with the attention-directing view; then 'Boston' in (10) is used to direct attention to a certain word spelled B O S T O N (or pronounced 'bawstun'). This use of 'Boston' both specifies and identifies the referent for the audience by presenting a sample of the word, and then this sample is related to the property of having six letters. Even though an RE is generally used to refer to something other than itself, it can be used to refer to itself. Moreover, such self-reference does not require a name of the RE, but can be accomplished by simply placing the RE in the discourse. It is difficult to place most things we want to talk about inside the discourse, but it is easily done for words (and for sounds, e.g., 'The car went bzzzz'). Even on this revised view, however, contexts within a quotation are not a counterexample to the principle of substitutivity, because the initial REs in (10) and (11) are not coreferential in this context, though they may be coreferential in others.

(B) Modal Contexts

Modal contexts also exhibit opacity. For these contexts, I will discuss SUB, but not quantification into them. A standard example from Quine (1961) is:

12. 9 is necessarily greater than 7.

13. The number of planets is necessarily greater than 7.

Though the substitution for '9' which forms (13) from (12) is invalid, other substitutions are valid in forming (14) and (15):

14. That number is necessarily greater than 7 [said with pointing to a certain numeral on a blackboard].

15. The positive square root of 81 is necessarily greater than 7.

Why is substitution invalid in producing (13), but valid in producing (14) and (15)? The empirical support for SUB came from the fact that the relating function in subject-predicate statements connects the object *qua* specified by the subject term with the property expressed by the predicate. Modal contexts disrupt this extensional contribution to truth conditions because the claim of necessity relates what is expressed by the subject RE to different possible worlds. If the subject RE is a non-rigid designator, it refers to whatever possesses a certain property, and different individuals may possess that property in different possible worlds. This explains the non-rigidity of the RE 'the number of planets' in (13). In contrast, a designator which functions on the figure-ground model determines a referent by a relation to the context of its use in the actual world, and not by relations to alternative possible worlds.

This explains the rigidity of the use of the RE 'that number' in (14). This account of rigidity was developed in chapter 2, but it can be supplemented by a feature of the tripartite model for reference from chapter 6, namely, the distinction between specifying the referent and relating it to other things. This allows for the specification of reference to occur in relation to the actual world, while the relating function brings in alternative possible worlds. If reference were a unitary function, it would operate either in relation to the actual world or in relation to alternative possible circumstances, but not in relation to both.

A different account is needed for the validity of substituting 'the positive square root of 81' for '9' so as to produce (15), but this account exists already in the literature: the new description gives an essence of 9 which is true of it in all possible worlds.

(C) Contexts of Propositional Attitude[16]

The most recalcitrant opaque contexts are those involving propositional attitudes, for example:

16. John believes that the first person born in Sun City in 1898 is a spy.

Suppose that the first person born in Sun City in 1898 is identical to the heaviest drinker at the party. We cannot validly conclude to

17. John believes that the heaviest drinker at the party is a spy.

In such contexts, REs seem to make a semantic contribution in addition to their extension. Given the earlier hypothesis that SUB was based on the point that simple subject-predicate statements direct attention to a thing *qua* specified as related to other things in discourse, we might expect that the means of specifying reference is itself related to something in the discourse, so as to affect the truth conditions. But attitudinal contexts may also affect EG. Maybe no one was born in Sun City in 1898, so that EG would also be invalid on 'the first person born in Sun City in 1898.' What are the mechanisms by which attitudinal contexts affect EG and SUB? To discuss this within the limits of the present book, I must restrict the topic in several ways. First, I shall focus on linguistic issues of opacity and transparency, and set aside related psychological issues. Second, I shall talk only about beliefs, even though there is a wide range of propositional attitudes (e.g., hopes, fears, dislikes, etc.). Third, the examples I shall discuss involve only indexicals and definite descriptions. Fourth, I shall omit examples in which the speaker and the subject of the attitude are the same person.

Since attitudinal contexts interact with reference to produce opacity, I shall use the attention-directing models as part of my account. However, to apply the models to the problem, we must also understand the basic mechanisms of attitudinal contexts. I suggest that their key feature, in relation to opacity, is that they are *reports*.[17] In most contexts, a speaker takes full responsibility for his assertions and his references. However, in attitudinal contexts, because the speaker is reporting either his own or someone else's beliefs, he need not take full responsibility for reported assertions or references. Concerning such reports, two roles can be distinguished:[18] those of the speaker and of the subject of the propositional attitude; for brevity, I refer to the latter as the reportee. These two roles may bear different relations to the use of an RE inside an attitudinal context, and these different relations affect the functioning of ways of specifying reference, thereby affecting opacity and transparency. This is why contexts of propositional attitude are so difficult: reference within them interacts with *two distinct contextual factors* that have independent effects on opacity and transparency, whereas in most other types of opaque contexts, just one contextual factor interacts with reference. There are two kinds of relations of REs to speakers and reportees that affect opacity in attitudinal contexts:

(a) an RE may be used *to make the speaker's reference*.[19]

or

(b) an RE may be used *to report the way that the reportee specifies a referent*,

or

(c) *both* (a) and (b) may occur together. (In this case, the speaker makes the same reference as the reportee is reported to make.)

If the speaker uses an RE to make his own reference, then he is usually also vouching for the existence of the referent; this affects EG. If the speaker uses an RE to report how the reportee specifies a referent, then the report thereby includes the way the reportee thinks about the referent in specifying it. But then a coreferential substitute for the RE is unlikely to describe the reportee's thinking in the same way; this affects SUB.

The relations (a) and (b) connect uses of REs with speakers

and reportees respectively. The relations (a) and (b) themselves are
related as follows. If an RE is not used to report a belief of the
reportee about a way of specifying reference, then it must be used
to make the speaker's reference. This is because a speaker, in
using an RE within an attitudinal context, has to produce at least
one of the relations (a) or (b). But a speaker may produce both of
these relations as in (c). Such double functioning can occur in the
use of an indexical RE in an attitudinal context.

Based on these relations of uses of REs to speaker and reportee, I have developed two rules for transparency and opacity in
attitudinal contexts, as well as hypotheses about the mechanisms
underlying the rules.

Preliminary Version of Rule 1:
For EG to be valid on an RE within attitudinal contexts, the RE
must be used to make the speaker's reference.

Consider an example:

18.   Harold believes that this tree will die soon.

18 A. $(\exists x)[(x$ is a tree) and (Harold believes $(x$ will die soon$))]$

The validity of EG in relation to an RE in a sentence requires that
a claim of existence is justified by prior claims. But only the
speaker is making a claim in an attitudinal context. The reportee's
claim is not made, but is instead reported. Therefore, only the
speaker's reference can support EG, because only it is presupposed
by a person making a claim in the context. In (18), the speaker
took responsibility for the reference of 'this tree' in (18) by making
a claim that presupposes this reference. This presupposition is
what supports the application of EG to such a context.[20]

This rule for EG is only a preliminary version, however, because of the kinds of REs within attitudinal contexts for whose
reference the speaker takes responsibility. The only such REs
(given our prior limitation to indexicals and definite descriptions),
for which *Rule 1* holds are indexicals and referentially used descriptions. Attributively used descriptions, when they are *inside*
the scope of the attitudinal verb at the surface level, are used to
report how the reportee specifies the referent, and not to make the
speaker's reference.[21] This occurs because attributively used descriptions function on the *predication* model, so that the speaker
reports a belief of the reportee concerning *whatever is the one and
only F*. But being *F* is being a member of a kind which provides the

means for specifying the referent. Thus, an RE used on the predication model inside the scope of an attitudinal verb produces a report of how the reportee specifies the referent, for example:

19. Harold believes that the winner of the next lottery will be a professional gambler.

In (19), the report includes the point that Harold specifies the referent as winner of the next lottery. On the other hand, if an attributively used description is at the surface level *outside* the scope of an attitudinal verb, the speaker specifies the referent, and need not report how the reportee specifies it; for example, suppose that the initial RE is attributively used in the following:

20. The winner of the lottery is in the next room, and Harold believes she is a professional gambler.

In contrast, when the figure-ground model is used within an attitudinal context, the speaker takes responsibility (unless there is a disclaimer) for the reference, because he, and not the reportee, directs the hearer's attention to a thing, and the speaker does so by using his own gestures and context. If a speaker reports a belief about a thing *qua* particular without reporting how the reportee specifies the referent, he may pick out the referent *qua* particular with no consideration of how the reportee would do so. The figure-ground model (but not the predication model) allows such a report for REs located inside the scope of an attitudinal verb.

Now we can see why *Rule 1* needs to be more restricted than the preliminary version. Because this rule is applicable (in our restricted range of examples) only to REs functioning on the figure-ground model, and because descriptions functioning on that model function perceptually, there is a problem for EG. EG uses quantification, which requires a predicative description to quantify over, but descriptions function *perceptually* on the figure-ground model, and need not be true of their referents. Therefore, there is a problem about what to quantify over when EG is applied to an indexical. I repeat the earlier example and application of EG:

21.   Harold believes that this tree will die soon.
21 A. $(\exists x)[(x$ is a tree) and (Harold believes $(x$ will die soon$))]$

The problem here is that the speaker of (21) may vouch for the reference of 'this tree' in (21) on the figure-ground model, while not vouching for the point that the description 'tree' is true of the referent. Perhaps the speaker knows that it is really a bush, and not a tree. Then the speaker would not vouch for (21 A) even though he did vouch for the reference he made by 'this tree' in (21). We could imagine the speaker saying (22) immediately after (21):

22. But this is a bush, not a tree.

But (22) plus (21 A) is a contradiction. To avoid the possibility of inferring such contradictions by EG, we need to restrict *Rule 1* as follows:

> *Second Version of Rule 1:*
> For EG to be valid on an RE within attitudinal contexts, the RE must be used to make the speaker's reference, and any descriptions within the RE must be left inside the belief report.

Applying this rule to (21) yields

21 B. ($\exists$x)[Harold believes (x is a tree) and (x will die soon)]

But this conclusion also fails to follow from the premise. Here the problem is that (21 B) reports that Harold specifies reference to the thing by the predicate 'tree,' and this was not present in (21); it may be that Harold thinks of it as a bush also. Therefore, we have to change *Rule 1* again:

> *Final Version of Rule 1:*
> For EG to be valid on an RE within attitudinal contexts, the RE must be used to make the speaker's reference, and any descriptions within the RE must be dropped.

On this version, the application of EG to (21) yields

21 C. ($\exists$x)[Harold believes (x will die soon)]

This is an extreme restriction, but it seems required. I must also mention that *Rule 1* does not assure the validity of EG in attitudinal contexts, because there are many other factors which affect EG besides attitudinal contexts, and these might be present within an attitudinal context.

The validity of EG in attitudinal contexts depends on whether the speaker takes responsibility for the reference, but this does not affect the validity of SUB. It instead is affected by whether the speaker uses the RE to report the reportee's way of specifying the referent. The relevant rule is

> *Preliminary Version of Rule 2:*
> For SUB to be valid, on an RE within attitudinal contexts, the specification of reference by the replacement RE must *not* be used to report the reportee's way of specifying the referent.

Consider an example:

23. John believes that that man next to the punch bowl is a spy.

24. John believes that that man who has the loud sport coat and is smoking a pipe is a spy.

Suppose that (24) is derived from (23) by substitution of coreferential demonstrative phrases. This inference would be valid in the following case. Suppose that John is not at the party, and the speaker in (23) is using 'that man next to the punch bowl' to make his own reference, and not to report how John thinks about the referent. Thus, he reports John's belief concerning this individual, but not how the reportee specifies reference to him. Suppose then that 'that man next to the punch bowl' is coreferential in the context with 'that man in the loud sport coat and smoking a pipe.' Then the latter RE, if it is not used to report how the reportee specifies the referent, can be substituted for the former, *salva veritate*. In this example, the speaker is reporting a belief of the reportee about a certain person without reporting how the reportee specifies that person.[22]

If a replacement description were used to report the reportee's way of specifying the referent, the resulting report would be unwarranted by (23). An example of such a case would be a conclusion from (23) to

25. John believes that the heaviest drinker at the party is a spy.

Suppose that 'that man next to the punch bowl' and 'the heaviest drinker at the party' are coreferential in the context. Nevertheless, the substitution that produces (25) from (23) would be invalid, because the RE 'the heaviest drinker at the party' is used attributively, and thus specifies as its referent whatever it is true of. This last point entails that in an attitudinal context, the description in the RE describes how the reportee specifies the referent. Therefore, attributive uses of REs within an attitudinal context always describe how the reportee specifies the referent. But (23) does not support the point that John specifies the referent as the heaviest drinker at the party. For this reason, *Rule 2* stipulates that the replacement RE not be used to report the reportee's way of specifying reference.[23]

Unfortunately, the preliminary version of *Rule 2* is inadequate because it allows invalid inferences. Consider an example:

26. Harold believes that the oldest faculty member will be given an offer to retire which he cannot refuse.

Suppose that 'the oldest faculty member' is coreferential in the context with 'that man holding a cat.' The result of substitution into (26) would be

27. Harold believes that that man holding a cat will be given an offer to retire which he cannot refuse.

Suppose that the replacement RE 'that man holding a cat' is not used to report how the reportee specifies the referent. Then the substitution is valid according to the preliminary version of *Rule 2*. Harold's belief as reported in (26), however, is a general one about whoever is the oldest faculty member; it says nothing about a person *qua* particular. Harold might also believe that a certain individual (the one pointed out in (27) as holding at cat) is in fact the oldest faculty member, but such a belief is not reported in (26). Since (27) indicates that Harold has a belief about a person *qua* particular, whereas such a belief is not indicated by (26), (26) does not entail (27). Therefore, to avoid deducing a belief report about a thing *qua* particular from a report about a thing *qua* member of a kind, *Rule 2* needs a restriction as follows:

> *Final Version of Rule 2:*
> For SUB to be valid on an RE within attitudinal contexts, the specification of reference by the replacement RE must *not* be used to report the reportee's way of specifying the referent, and the original RE must be used to make the speaker's reference.

When the original RE is used within the scope of the attitudinal operator to make the speaker's reference, it must make *qua* particular reference. Since the replacement RE must make *qua* particular reference also, we avoid the problem in the derivation of (27), that of deducing a belief report about an individual *qua* particular from a belief report about an individual *qua* member of a kind. In parallel with *Rule 1*, the present rule does not guarantee that SUB is valid, because factors other than attitudinal contexts can affect SUB. Rather, the point of the rule is that as far as attitudinal contexts by themselves are considered, SUB is valid.

There is another conceivable way to attempt to avoid the implication that Harold's belief in (27) was about a particular individual; one could place the substituted RE outside the attitudinal operator, thus yielding one of these two statements:

28. Concerning that man holding a cat, Harold believes that he will be given an offer to retire which he cannot refuse.

29. There is one and only one man around here holding a cat, and
    Harold believes that he will be given an offer to retire which
    he cannot refuse.

There are two problems with these applications of SUB. First, they
are invalidly derived from (26), since one implies and the other
asserts the existence of a man holding a cat, whereas such an implication or claim was not present in (26) because 'the oldest faculty member' was used to report the reportee's way of specifying
reference, and not to make the speaker's reference. The speaker
might know on other grounds that there is one and only one oldest
faculty member, but this point is not required by the belief report
given in (26). The second problem is that (28) and (29) might still
imply that Harold has a belief about the person *qua* individual, or
qua man holding a cat, despite the fact that at the surface level the
new REs are outside the scope of the attitudinal operator. Quine
himself (1960: 150) speaks of "our conventions" in regard to some
of the regimentation that he uses to mark opacity and transparency in attitudinal contexts. Sentences in natural language are not
regimented, and instead have meanings that are influenced by contexts.

An RE can be used both to make the speaker's reference and to
report how the reportee specifies reference, and in one kind of context, an RE must be so used, namely, in attitudinal contexts with
embedded identity statements whose REs are indexicals, for example:

30. John believes that that man whose back is reflected in the mir-
    ror is you.

Because the indexical references in (30) are constituted by the
speaker's attention directing in relation to the physical surroundings, he takes responsibility for the references unless he indicates
the contrary. But the REs inside the attitudinal context are also
being used to report how the reportee specifies the referent. This is
shown by the fact that if they were not used for this purpose, and
instead contributed only their extensions to the report, then the
reported belief would have no more informative content than the
statement,

31. John believes that you are you.

Clearly, (30) has more content that (31). The REs inside the report
in (30) must contribute their ways of specifying reference to the
proposition because they are also inside an identity context, within

which two ways of specifying reference are said to specify the same thing. Since the identity context is subordinated to the attitudinal context, the identity context is used to report a belief that two particular ways of specifying reference specify a certain thing.[24]

De Dicto vs. *De Re* Uses of Referring Expressions

The traditional distinction between *de dicto* and *de re* uses of terms has been drawn for both modal and attitudinal contexts. In both, *de re* uses indicate a *primacy of individual things*, whereas *de dicto* uses indicate a *primacy of descriptions* of things. I propose to draw the distinction on a principled basis which describes the interaction of the mechanism of reference with modal and attitudinal contexts. If the way of specifying reference expressed by a use of an RE determines a referent and relates to the modal or attitudinal context only through that referent, then the RE is used *de re*,[25] whereas if the way of specifying reference functions in relation to the modal or attitudinal context, then the RE is used *de dicto*. Despite these similarities in origin, the *de re* vs. *de dicto* distinctions are rather different for modal and attitudinal contexts, for reasons which will become clear.

A modal operator relates a proposition to alternative possible circumstances of evaluation. If the way of specifying reference expressed by an RE determines its referent before such relating, and relates to the alternative possible worlds only through its referent, then the RE is used *de re*. Such a specification of reference is produced by indexical reference, because the figure-ground model specifies a referent in relation to the actual world before possible worlds come into play. To repeat an earlier example:

32. That number is necessarily greater than 7 [said with pointing to a certain numeral on a blackboard].

If the way of specifying reference expressed by an RE does not determine its referent before relating to alternative possible worlds, it determines its referent in relation to them, for example:

33. The number of planets is necessarily greater than 7.

Because the initial RE in (33) functions on the predication model, it refers to whatever the description is true of, and within a modal context this results in specifying reference in relation to alternative possible worlds. Thus, the way of specifying reference functions in immediate relation to the modal context, so that a *de dicto* use results.

For propositional attitudes, *de re* uses can (but need not) be produced by the functioning of REs on the figure-ground model. The important question about *de re* status for uses of REs in attitudinal contexts is not whether the REs determine reference in relation to the actual world (or are rigid designators), but rather whether they are used to report a belief of the reportee about a way of specifying reference. If an RE is so used, the use is *de dicto*, and if it is not so used, the use is *de re*. I repeat an earlier example:

34. John believes that that man next to the punch bowl is a spy.

Suppose that (34) is used at a party and that John is not there. In such a context, the report concerns John's belief about the individual *qua* particular, but nothing is reported about how John specifies this individual. In this situation, the way of specifying reference expressed by 'that man next to the punch bowl' is not used to report the reportee's way of specifying the referent, so that the use is *de re*. This *de re* status fits our intuitions, in that the report is about the thing *qua* particular no matter how it might be specified by the subject of the attitude. In contrast, in a *de dicto* use, the RE is used to report the way in which the subject of the attitude specifies the referent, for example:

35. Harold believes that the oldest faculty member will be given an offer to retire which he cannot refuse.

Intuitively, the RE 'the oldest faculty member' is used *de dicto* because it is used to describe how the reportee specifies the referent. In attitudinal contexts, however, *de dicto* uses of REs can result not only from REs functioning on the predication model, but also from REs that specify reference on the figure-ground model, as long as they are also used to report a belief of the subject of the attitude about away of specifying reference. Again I repeat an example:

36. John believes that that man whose back is reflected in the mirror is you.

The indexical REs in (36) are used *de dicto* even though they determine their referents in relation to the physical surroundings in the actual world, and even though the speaker and hearer perceive the referent *qua* particular; the belief report is not just about the referent no matter how he is described, but rather about the referent as picked out in certain ways.

The present accounts of the *de re/de dicto* distinction for REs in modal and attitudinal contexts are quite unified; the differences between the accounts result from the natures of those contexts. Because modal contexts bring in relations to alternative possible circumstances, the primacy of a thing over descriptions in relation to possible worlds is constituted by determining the thing in relation to the actual world only. Because attitudinal contexts produce reports of beliefs, the primacy of a thing in relation to such a report is constituted by using an RE to specify a thing which is mentioned in the report, without using the way of specifying reference to report the reportee's belief about a way of determining reference.

(D) Attribute-Identity Contexts

Quine (1961: 156–157) suggests that contexts involving the idiom 'the attribute of being . . .' are opaque. The examples he gives are cases in which such idioms are used in identity contexts; therefore, I call such cases 'attribute-identity contexts,' for example:

37. The attribute of exceeding 9 = the attribute of exceeding 9.

Quine argues that substitution of a coreferential RE in (37) produces the falsehood

38. The attribute of exceeding the number of the planets = the attribute of exceeding 9.

Since (38) is clearly false, the substitution which produced it must be invalid, and thus (37) appears to be opaque. Quine ascribes the opacity of (37) to the fact that it is an attribute context, but he offers no account of how such contexts produce opacity, though he (1961: 157) does assimilate them to modal sentences, and points out that attributes are intensional entities.

My general account of identity statements provides a basis for explaining opacity in attribute-identity contexts. On my general view, identity contexts are used to claim to that two ways of specifying reference specify a certain thing referred to by one of them. My analysis for (38) would be

38 A. W (expressed by 'attribute of exceeding 9') and W (expressed by 'attribute of exceeding the number of planets') specify the attribute of exceeding 9.

Because attributes correspond closely to the ways in which they are specified, usually two different ways of specifying attributes will specify different attributes. However, there are two exceptions to this general rule: first, if the two ways of specifying the attribute are synonymous, and second, if the two ways of specifying the attribute specify the same attribute according to an empirical law, for example:

39. The attribute of being secretary to an oculist = the attribute of being secretary to an ophthalmologist.

40. The attribute of raising the temperature of a gas = the attribute of raising the mean kinetic energy of a gas.

In the first case, the attributes involved are the same despite the difference in words because the words 'oculist' and 'ophthalmologist' mean the same, and therefore specify the same attribute. In the second case, the attributes involved are the same despite the difference in the meanings of the words because there is a well-confirmed empirical theory according to which these two different ways of specifying an attribute expressed by 'temperature' and 'mean kinetic energy' specify the same attribute.[26] But in the absence of either logical equivalence (as in (39)) or identity of attributes within an empirical theory (as in (40)), different ways of specifying things specify them on the basis of attributes that are different. Since an identity statement like (38) claims that attributes are the same, and since the attributes referred to by the substituted terms are not the same on the basis of either synonymy or an empirical law, the substitution that produced (38) is invalid. Because the REs involved in the substitution are not coreferential in the context ('9' refers to one attribute, and 'the number of planets' refers to a different attribute when one is talking about attributes, as in (38)), it follows that the principle of substitutivity has not been violated. Therefore, one may wish to call such cases 'apparently opaque contexts.' After all, genuinely coreferential REs as in (39) and (40) do allow substitution in a context of attribute-identity.

(E) Proposition-Identity Contexts

Contexts of the form, 'the proposition that . . .,' which are embedded in an identity claim, are taken by Quine (1961: 157) to be opaque. For example, consider:

41. The proposition that $9 > 7$ = the proposition that $9 > 7$.

42. The proposition that the number of planets > 7 = the proposition that $9 > 7$.

Quine argues that since (42) is obtained from (41) by substitution on the basis of the true identity of 9 and the number of planets, and since (42) is false while (41) is true, an opaque context must be present. He assimilates this opacity to that of attribute contexts.

There are both similarities and differences between attribute-identity and propositional-identity contexts. The similarity is that just as materially equivalent REs like 'the number of planets' and '9' specify different attributes, so also they make different contributions to the propositions containing them, so that the RE 'the proposition that the number of planets > 7' has a different referent from the RE 'The proposition that 9 > 7.' My analysis of (42) is

42 A. W (expressed by 'proposition that the number of planets > 7') and W (expressed by 'proposition that 9 > 7') specify the proposition that the number of planets > 7.

Because of the different ways of specifying reference contributed by '9' and 'the number of planets,' (42 A) is false.

Proposition-identity contexts, however, also differ from attribute-identity contexts. The contents of propositions are directly affected by the ways of specifying reference which REs contribute to them, whereas the identity of attributes is not directly affected by ways of specifying reference; instead, the ways of specifying reference pick out attributes which are contributed to the attribute-identity claim. Suppose that certain ways of specifying reference pick out the same attribute either because of logical equivalence or empirical laws. Then these ways of specifying reference make the same contribution to a claim about *attributes*, but different contributions to a claim about *propositions*. The latter point holds even when the ways of specifying reference are intentionally isomorphic (cf. Mates (1950) and Partee (1973)), for example:

43. The proposition that an oculist is here = the proposition that an oculist is here.

44. The proposition that an oculist is here = the proposition that an ophthalmologist is here.

Even though 'an ophthalmologist' is logically equivalent to and intensionally isomorphic with 'an oculist,' the substitution is invalid because each provides a different way of specifying reference,[27] and proposition-identity contexts make claims about propositions which are partially constituted by ways of specifying reference. Therefore, substitution of REs is invalid in proposition-identity contexts because even logically equivalent REs express different ways of specifying reference. Again, this is not a violation of the principle of substitutivity, since even logically equivalent REs, when used to refer to ways of specifying reference, are not coreferential.

(F) Assertions of Non-Existence

Contexts involving an assertion of non-existence are opaque in regard to EG, but not in regard to SUB. Consider an example:

45. There is no such thing as that sta-puff marshmallow monster.

46. There is an x such that there is no such thing as x.

Suppose that (45) is said to a child who has just seen the movie *Ghostbusters*. Quine (1961: 145) points out that inferences like the one from (45) to (46) are invalid. Though he does not explicitly call a context like (45) opaque, it fits his criterion of quantification: one cannot quantify into this context. However, one can validly substitute in such contexts, for example:

47. There is no such thing as the monster sent to destroy New York near the end of the movie *Ghostbusters*.

Thus, Quine's two criteria of opacity produce different results in this case.

In the early part of this chapter, an account of the workings of existence statements was based on the attention-directing model for reference. This theory of reference can also be used to explain why substitution can be valid even though existential generalization is not. The RE 'the monster sent to destroy New York near the end of the movie *Ghostbusters*' directs attention to the same thing that the original RE directed attention to. In the context of existence claims (and denials), REs that direct attention to the same thing will be substitutable *salva veritate* because the existence claim (or denial) will have the same truth value no matter how the thing is referred to.

(G) Contexts of Production[28]

Contexts that concern production are opaque according to the criterion of existential generalization, but transparent according to the criterion of substitutivity, for example:

48. John is building a model of the Eiffel Tower.

Suppose that a model of Eiffel Tower is identical with a small replica of the tallest structure in Paris; then it follows from (48) by the principle of substitutivity that

49. John is building a small replica of the tallest structure in Paris.

But from (48) it does not follow that

50. There is an x such that x is a model of the Eiffel Tower and John is building x.

Statement (48) can be analyzed as containing a use of 'a model of the Eiffel Tower' to make nonspecific reference, that is, reference to a thing as one member of a kind (without restricting it to being the only member of the kind). Such reference by itself does not require that the particular thing exist; rather, attention is directed to a thing of that kind as related to other objects of attention-directing. The other objects, in this example, are John and his activity of building. When a model is related as the object of the activity of building, the model is in the process of coming into existence. Until this process is completed, or almost completed, the model does not exist, with the result that EG need not be valid on 'a model.'

   In the past tense (e.g., 'he built a ship'), the RE 'a ship' usually has an existing referent, but the present tense in (48) carries no such implication. Though it may seem objectionable to postulate a difference in the functioning of the object of a verb merely because of a difference in the verb's tense, this difference is important for a verb like 'build': when the action of building is completed, the result is (usually, but more than logic is involved)[29] the existence of what was built, whereas when the action of building is going on, the product does not yet exist (or exists only partially). Therefore, introduction of a thing into discourse *qua* member of a kind does not by itself require the existence of the thing; whether or not there is a supposition that a thing so introduced exists depends on the nature of the verb and other factors in the context that the RE is related to.

   The second way to analyze (48) is to view the RE 'a model of the Eiffel Tower' not as a referring expression, but rather as forming a compound with the verb, so that the latter becomes 'is Eiffel-Tower-model-building':

48 A. John is Eiffel-Tower-model-building.'

Neither interpretation of (48) requires that the particular thing exist. The two analyses specify the type of production with differing emphases: the first emphasizes the product, and brings in non-specific reference to a member of the kind as the product, whereas the second emphasizes the activity of production, and brings in reference to the kind but not to a member of it. Because of this difference, (48) states that John is working on a single model; (48 A) lacks this point, because it focuses more on the activity and less on the product.

Some verbs other than production verbs also do not require the existence of their objects, for example:

51. John does not own a boat.

Non-ownership does not require the existence of the thing that is not owned. Here as in (48), the verb and object can be formed into a compound predicate:

51 A. John is not a boat-owner.

(H) Adjectives Which Cast Doubt on Existence or Genuineness

Modifiers like 'apparent,' 'pretend,' 'fake,' and 'counterfeit' can block existential generalization, for example:

52. The apparent oasis is on the left.

The use of existential generalization on (52) would not be reasonable, since it would involve commitment to an entity which the original statement was not committed to. Even though existential generalization is not valid here, substitution seems to be valid, for example:

52 A. The apparent watering place is on the left.

The attention-directing model handles such examples with ease, since the descriptive term 'oasis' has its usual attention directing function, and the modifier 'apparent' has an evaluative function, casting doubt on whether there really is a referent fitting the description.

(I) Nouns Whose Content Precludes Existential Generalization

REs like 'the ghost' do not allow existential generalization in most contexts, but they do allow substitution, for example:

53. The ghost of Tarnish Tower has not been seen for 100 years.

In (53), there is no indication whether the speaker is committed to the existence of the ghost or not, so that it is unclear whether or not existential generalization would be valid. I argued at the beginning of my study of opacity that the validity of EG does not follow from the mere use of an RE to refer, but rather from that use plus the speaker's supposition that the referent exists. Thus, the application to natural language of the rule of EG has a statistical basis in the fact that people usually use REs to refer to things whose existence they presuppose. But the meaning of the word 'ghost,' in conjunction with the background beliefs of our society about ghosts, makes it at least questionable whether the speaker would be presupposing the existence of the ghost. Whether or not EG is valid here depends on nonlogical matters, namely, the speaker's beliefs about ghosts.

(J) Ambiguity-Producing Substitutions

SUB fails to be truth preserving when the substituted RE produces an ambiguity, for example:

54. Jane gave the comptroller of the bank his bike.

55. The president of the bank gave the comptroller of the bank his bike.

Suppose that 'Jane' and 'the president of the bank' are coreferential. The substitution of the coreferential RE in (55) fails to be truth preserving because it renders 'his' in (55) ambiguous, whereas it was not ambiguous in (54). The attention-directing view of reference casts some light on this case: REs do not merely bring a referent into discourse; they also specify the referent by means of their content. 'Jane' and 'the president of the bank' differ in the way that each specifies its referent (in that the former has gender information that the latter lacks), and this information is needed to disambiguate a later anaphorical reference.

(K) Gareth Evans' E-type Anaphora

Gareth Evans' (1977 in 1980) E-type anaphora involves a pronoun to which existential generalization cannot be applied, for example:

56. John owns some sheep and Harry vaccinates them.

57. Few MP's came to the party, but they had a marvelous time.

Because 'them' in (56) and 'they' in (57) cannot be represented by means of quantified REs whose quantifier ranges over both the pronoun and its apparent antecedent, these pronouns are in a context which cannot be quantified into from outside. Therefore, on Quine's quantificational definition of opacity, such contexts are opaque. (But SUB would be valid.) The opacity in these cases derives from the fact that these pronouns are not coreferential with antecedent REs, but instead refer to things talked about by means of whole clauses: 'John owns some sheep' or 'Few MP's came to the party.' The failure of 'them' is (56) to be coreferential with an antecedent RE is surprising if one views anaphora as a syntactic matter of coreferential REs, but if one instead views it as a semantic-pragmatic matter of using a figure to search the discourse dependent context, the surprise is removed. On the latter view, 'them' in (56) picks out what was talked about by means of the whole clause 'John owns some sheep,' namely, the sheep that John owns. Discourse contexts contain not only individuals, but also groups and situations that were talked about, whether or not they were referred to by means of REs.

The varieties of opacity discussed so far all derive their opacity from the referential functioning of RES, whereas the next four varieties of opacity arise from using the contents of REs in an additional way, beyond referential functioning.

(L) Emphasis-selecting Words

Contrastive underlinings produce opacity in regard to substitutivity, but not existential generalization. For example:

58. Socrates' *drinking hemlock* at dusk caused his death.

59. Socrates's drinking hemlock *at dusk* caused his death.

Even though the initial five-word REs that provide the subjects of (58) and (59) are coreferential, they cannot be substituted *salva veritate* in the given context. Peter Achinstein provides the following account of how the underlining produces opacity:

> How, then, does emphasis yield opacity in causal contexts? It does so via the phenomenon of *semantical aspect-selectivity*. An emphasized word or phrase in a nominalized cause term of a causal statement is selected as expressing an aspect of the situation that is causally operative. A shift in emphasis shifts the causally oper-

ative aspect and thus changes the meaning, and hence possibly
the truth-value of the resulting claim. (1979: 370)

Achinstein holds, correctly in my opinion, that opacity in cases like
(58) derives from a number of emphasis-selecting words that gener-
ate opaque contexts (e.g., 'explain,' 'reason,' 'dangerous,' 'illegal,'
'important' (1979: 372)). Such words pick up on the contrast produced by underlining so that truth conditions are affected. The contrast produced by the underlining in (58) and (59) is roughly this:

58 A. It was the drinking of hemlock, and not the fact that it was
       at dusk that Socrates did it, that caused his death.[30]

59 A. It was the fact that it was at dusk that Socrates did some-
       thing, and not that what he did was to drink hemlock, that
       caused his death.

I will add to Achinstein's account a brief explanation of the
underlying conditions in examples like (58) and (59). In these examples, the underlining functions to put some terms to *double use*.
The first use is referential, to specify (with the help of other terms)
a referent and relate it to other things in discourse. The second use
is to specify a property that underlies the causal relation. If one
holds that causation involves a law in some way, and if one holds
with Fred I. Dretske (1977) that laws involve relations of properties, then one can view the underlining in (58) as picking out a
property of an action as related by a law to a result (drinking hemlock causes death). On this account of (58), the following para-
phrase makes clear its logical structure:

58 B. Socrates' drinking hemlock at dusk caused his death, and it
       was the property of drinking hemlock that made this action
       causative of his death.

The substitution which produces (59) is invalid because it names a
different property as the cause of Socrates' death.

(M) Reflexive Pronouns

Certain contexts that involve reflexive pronouns are opaque in
regard to substitutivity, but not in regard to existential generalization, for example:

60. Only John shot himself in the foot at the rifle meet.[31]

That (60) is opaque is shown by the failure of substitutivity for
'himself':

60 A. Only John shot John in the foot at the rifle meet.

Suppose that Harold also shot John in the foot at the meet. Then (60) would be true while (60 A) is false. Therefore, (60) is opaque.

The opacity of 'himself' in (60) occurs because this reflexive pronoun has another role in addition to that of referring. In English, a reflexive pronoun like 'himself' is used to change a predicate like 'shoot' into a compound predicate 'is a self-shooter.'[32] In some languages, for example, Greek, such predicates are syntactically marked not by reflexive pronouns, but by verbs in a middle voice (which is in addition to the active and passive voices). This syntactic fact about middle voices supports the view that reflexive pronouns function not only as referring expressions but also as modifying the functioning of the verb with which they are used. Substitution in (60) is not truth preserving because it changes this compound predicate, 'is a self-shooter,' into a simple predicate plus an object, and the latter combination has different truth conditions in the given context.

Existential generalization over the initial RE of (60) is valid, as long as the reflexivity of the propositional function is retained. Using 'Sxy for 'x shot y,' the quantified version of (60) is

60 B. $(\exists x)$ (Sxx and (y)[Syy $\supset$ (x = y)])[33]

Reflexive propositional functions require the same variable in at least two places; if this requirement is not followed, an invalid quantification of (60) would result, for example:

60 C. $(\exists x)$ [Sxx and (y)[Syx $\supset$ (x = y)]]

Since (60 C), like (60 A), could be false while (60) is true (e.g., in the case where Harold also shot John in the foot), this way of quantifying (60) is invalid.

(N) The Order of Narration

Contexts in which the order of narration of an RE affects the truth-value of the proposition also produce opacity in regard to substitutivity, but not existential generalization:

61.   The plane gradually descended from the east over the landmarks of New Jersey, Delaware, and Maryland, as it approached the Washington, D.C. airport.

61 A. The plane gradually descended from the east over the landmarks of Delaware, Maryland, and New Jersey, as it approached the Washington, D.C. airport.

This substitution of a coreferential RE for 'the landmarks of New Jersey, Delaware, and Maryland' in (61) is not truth preserving because a *gradual* descent to Washington, D.C. from the east requires exactly this order of states. Thus, in addition to referential functions, the RE in question serves to indicate an order of descent by means of the order of narration. Here again, existential generalization is truth preserving, for example:

61 B.   There are x such that x are landmarks of three states, New Jersey, Delaware, and Maryland, and the plane gradually descended from the east over x as it approached the Washington, D.C. airport.

(O) Setting a Standard for Comparison

David Houghton (1987: 141) also suggests that a description may both refer to a particular individual and serve a non-referential purpose. His example is

62.   Smith is better than the country's leading wicket-taker.

Houghton then comments on substituting a coreferential description for 'the country's leading wicket-taker' as follows:

> Yet it would be logically permissible to substitute a different description which that individual also satisfied (e.g. 'the university's cleverest mathematician') only on condition that the field of comparison indicated by the original description, bowling ability, remained understood and that no new field of comparison (e.g. mathematical ability) was allowed to be imported by the substitute description. (1987: 141)

If we made the indicated substitution, the result is

63.   Smith is better than the university's cleverest mathematician.

and this does imply that what Smith is better at is mathematics. Therefore, substitutivity is invalid, though existential generalization is valid.

An Attempt to Put Some Order into the Varieties of Referential Opacity

The discussion of opaque contexts, like that of existence and identity contexts, was usually guided not just by truth conditions, but also by the purposes of the contexts. But some types of opacity reflect the basic functioning of reference, rather than some distinctive purpose in the context. In particular, types (J) and (K) reflect the basic nature of the *ground* in anaphorical reference on the figure-ground model. Such reference requires a background with structures in it so that a figure can pick things out of it by contrasts. But substitution of coreferential REs changes descriptions of that background (e.g., by removing gender information as in (55)), so that anaphorical pronouns whose functioning was based on that information cannot work. Another basic feature of anaphorical reference on the figure-ground model is that the ground is constituted by the discourse context, which contains words, stories, individuals, groups, and situations that are present or described in the discourse. This means that anaphora is not a mere matter of coreference with REs, but rather involves a search of the discourse context for things which can be picked out by a figure. Thus, one can refer to things that are talked about in the prior discourse, even though no single RE was used to refer to them as in (56).

Although speakers usually intend to refer to things that exist, this is not always the case. The varieties of opacity marked (F) through (I) indicate various means by which a speaker might set aside the supposition that an RE has a referent in the real world. These means are (F) an assertion of nonexistence; (G) using the RE as the object of a verb of production; (H) using in the RE adjectives which cast doubt on the reality of the referent; (I) using in the RE nouns (like 'ghost'), which the speaker does not take to have real referents. These cases are especially troublesome for an extensional view of reference, since they either deny or cast doubt on whether the RE has an extension.

More complex types of opacity occur when a speaker makes assertions that are not of simple subject-predicate form. These require a relating function in reference that differs from that of simple subject-predicate sentences. Such diverse relating functions are found in the varieties of opacity (A), (C), (D), and (E): For type (A), quotational contexts, the relating function picks up from the specificatory function the words themselves, and relates them to what the predicate expresses. The predicate of a sentence ('has five letters') provides a figure sufficient for indicating that the subject of the sentence picks out a term from the context, rather than its ordinary referent. This explains why the oral version of "'Boston' has five letters" is understood (with no phonetic representation of quotation marks). Attitudinal contexts, type (C), are complex, because belief reports allow two diverse but compatible uses to be made of REs (to report how the reportee specifies reference, and to make the speaker's reference). This allows the relating function to pick up either the way of specifying reference or a focus on what is picked out by the way of specifying reference. Types (D) and (E) combine identity contexts with reference to attributes and propositions. For (D), the relating function selects (from the specificatory function) attention-directing to attributes, and the identity proposition produces a claim that the two ways of directing attention pick out the same attribute. For (E), the relating function selects (from the specificatory function) the attention directings themselves, and the identity proposition produces a claim that the two ways of directing attention are the same.

Opacity of type (B), for modal contexts, resembles the types discussed in the previous paragraph in resulting from the interaction of reference with the context, but it is based on the specificatory function, rather than the relating function. REs functioning on the predication model specify their referents in relation to alternative possible circumstances, so that they direct attention to different things in different possible worlds. In contrast, an indexical RE specifies its referent in relation to the actual world only. This difference produces a failure of SUB in modal contexts for REs functioning on the predication model (unless they provide an essence) and allows SUB for rigidly designating REs.

In the types of opacity (L) through (O), a speaker uses REs with a double functioning, only one of which is referential. The other types of function are the following: for (L), providing a property that is used in an explanation; for (M), providing a reflexive predicate; for (N), providing an ordered set; for (O), providing an aspect for comparison. All of these examples allow EG, but not SUB because the latter changes the non-referential functioning of the RE.[34]

Summary

Existence and identity contexts, and transparent and opaque contexts, can be understood in terms of the interaction of the mechanisms of reference with the mechanisms of the various contexts.

Afterword

Since the attention-directing models were developed over many chapters and in response to a variety of issues, I thought it would be useful to present them in order from the more general to the less general. Also, I will suggest some wider implications of the models.

Summary of the Models for Reference

Reference, on my view, is constituted by three kinds of activity (a) identifying the referent for the audience, (b) specifying the referent for the purpose of relating an output from the specificatory function to other things in discourse, and (c) relating that output to those other things. All three activities and the relations to other things in discourse are matters of attention-directing. The specificatory function is a certain kind of attention-directing to a thing; within this function, there are two aspects, the attention-directing and its object, and either (or both) of these may be related to other things in discourse. Which of these is related by the relating function depends on the other end of the relation, which varies from subject-predicate contexts to existence and identity contexts, to attitudinal contexts, and so forth. And in addition to propositional *relata*, the output from the specificatory function may be related to expressions of emotion in interjections, or to the discourse as a whole as addressed to someone. Whether the relating function connects the attention-directing itself or its object to the other objects of attention-directing has important effects on transparency and opacity.

Both the specificatory and identificatory (I use 'identificatory' here as short for 'identificatory for the audience') functions may be carried out in various particular manners and by various particu-

143

lar means, though I have developed only two of each. The manners of reference treated are *qua* particular and *qua* member of a kind, and the means are the figure-ground model and the predication model. Reference on the predication model determines a referent in virtue of a description that is true of the referent, thereby producing the manner of reference that is *qua* member of a kind. Reference on the figure-ground model, in contrast, produces reference *qua* particular. This is a perceptual and social model, with three parts: the very use of an indexical directs the hearer's attention to the ground, that is, the context which contains the referent; actions and gestures (or descriptions) may direct the hearer's attention to a subsection of the context that contains the referent; a figure, provided by descriptions in the indexical phrase or in the discourse context, enables the hearer to pick out the referent by its contrast to the (narrowed) background. The ground for indexical reference is a threefold context, constituted by the physical surroundings, the discourse-dependent context, and the concerns of the conversers.

Definite descriptions may be used either referentially or attributively (or in other ways—my theory is incomplete here also). A referentially used description functions on the figure-ground model, and amounts to indexical reference to a thing, in any of the three kinds of contexts, that has already caught the notice of the conversers. An attributively used description functions on the predication model, with the added point that the referent is the only thing that fits the description.

Indefinite descriptions may be used either to make specific reference or to make nonspecific reference (or in other ways). Nonspecific reference is made to a single thing of a certain kind, say *F*, on the predication model, so that the manner of both specifying and identifying the referent is *qua* member of a kind. Such reference allows that more than one thing may be *F*, even though the reference is to a single *F*. But non-specific reference is not to a single *F qua* particular, because it leaves indeterminate which individual with the property *F* is the referent. Specific reference, in contrast, specifies a referent *qua* particular as far as manner is concerned. This is shown by the effects that negation or counterfactual contexts would have on the reference. But the use of the description in the context does not identify the referent *qua* particular for the audience. Thus, the specificatory functioning of an indefinite description used to make specific reference must be separate from its identificatory functioning. In fact, the specification of the referent need not be based on the speaker's own knowledge of the referent, but may instead have a social basis in the speaker's knowledge of other persons' talk about the referent. The identificatory function in specific reference is only partial, in that the referent is identified as having a certain property which is (usually) inadequate for picking out the referent in the context.

Wider Implications of the Models

The issues about methodology discussed in chapter I, and mentioned on occasion in the rest of the book, are not the main point of the book. The models are the main point. Nevertheless, the methodological issues are important. I came to realize this from various comments on my work (e.g., "This is pragmatics; it does not affect semantics." or "Why not rewrite it from the standpoint of Montague Grammar?"). The models cannot be understood apart from the goals and the methods used in developing them, and these can best be understood in contrast to currently predominant goals and methods.

A minimal implication of the models, in my opinion, is that they show the need for articulating structures in reference. An entity without structures is not understandable. But the preference for treating reference extensionally within the predicate-logic tradition, to say nothing of the direct reference theory, leaves reference without structure, or with predication as its only structure. Even if the attention-directing models are all wrong, some kinds of structures must be found to underlie reference if we are to understand it. And if we do not understand the workings of reference, we can hardly understand the workings of language in general, since reference provides important connections of language with the world and with other speakers.

Although the attention directing models cannot be transferred in any simple way to the reference of proper names or of natural kind terms (like 'dog' or 'water'), I think they cast some light on these issues. Description theories for proper names, that is, theories that take proper names to determine their referents by means of descriptions functioning as *predicates* which are true of the referent, have been thoroughly criticized by Kripke (1980) and Donnellan (1970). Causal chain theories, which many (e.g., Kripke (1980), Donnellan (1974), Devitt (1981), Berger (1989)) have used to replace description theories, are clearly short on positive content in that their *explanans* repeats the notion (reference by means of names) to be explained. For instance, causal chains for proper names are said to begin with the christening of an individual with a name, or by a use of a name to refer to a certain individual. Useful development of causal chain theories might be promoted by devising a complex of social-psychological and perceptual attention directings to explain (that is, to provide underlying ingredients and mechanisms for) the use of a name to refer to an individual. Another kind of aid for causal chain theories might be found in a parallel to specific reference made by means of indefinite descriptions. Such reference, as we saw in chapter 5, can occur in a case in which a user of the description cannot identify the referent on his own. This parallels the usual uses of names like 'Cicero' or 'Feynman.' Also, the distinction within specific reference between specification *qua* particular and identification *qua* member of a kind for the audience may have a parallel in some uses of proper names. Even though a name user need not be able to pick out our which individual is its referent, he usually needs to know some descriptive content associated with the referent of a proper name in order to use it correctly. For instance, in most contexts, a person will not use the name 'Mont Blanc' correctly if he does not know whether it is the name of a musical group or a mountain.

The attention directing family of models for reference also has implications beyond reference. Recall the three types of explanations of meaning that were discussed in chapter 1: the referential, ideational, and behavioral theories. Even though these fail as general theories of meaning, each is based on important facts about language: words are generally connected with ideas and behavior, and some words refer to things. All of these connections are problematical for model-theoretic semantics,[1] but built into the attention directing models. In addition, the latter make reference a social matter, so that it connects not only with the outside world, but also with other people.

The connections which the attention directing models provide between REs, things in the outside world, thought, behavior, and other people can provide foundations for dealing with major problems in recent philosophy. Consider three such problems. A breach has been developing recently between the semantics and psychology of reference (cf. Perry (1979) and Wettstein (1989)). A way to repair this breach can be found in the attention-directing models, because they connect the semantics of REs with psychological matters. A second problem in recent philosophy, which Tyler Burge (1979, 1986, 1990) has clarified and attacked, is individualism in linguistic and psychological theories. The attention-directing models, because they connect REs with things in the outside world and with other people, can help in remedying the overly individualistic nature of certain theories of language and psychology. A third major problem concerns realism in philosophy generally and in philosophy of science. Arguments abound for the conclusion that our language and thought do not connect us to things in an outside world, but rather to some sort of world of our own constructions. But these arguments are based on no other notion of reference than that of true description. Perhaps a socially and perceptually based notion of reference, which is not a matter of true description, can lend support to realism.

Notes

Chapter 1: An Introduction to Methodology

1. The *Cratylus* is an important source for this view.

2. I distinguish reference made by means of referring expressions (e.g., 'that dog' or 'the man') from the reference of terms (e.g., 'dog' or 'man') apart from their contribution to such expressions. Since my concern is with the former, I will usually use the term 'reference' to talk about it. I do not offer a definition of 'referring expression,' but instead trust that we can agree on enough examples of them to begin our study. I use the phrase 'referring expression' rather than 'noun phrase' because some referring expressions are single terms and not nouns (e.g., 'this,' 'now,' 'I').

3. I disagree with the view that only people, and not words, refer. I view REs as instruments by which people refer. When a principal cause uses an instrument to perform an action or produce a result, both the principle cause and the instrumental cause produce the action and the result, unless the action or result requires special mental features which the instrument lacks. For instance, guns kill (despite what the National Rifle Association says), but do not commit first degree murder. In the case of reference, both people and REs refer, the former as principal causes, and the latter as instrumental causes. I am not interested in the instrumental causality of REs by itself, but rather the entire process by which people use REs to refer.

4. Similar views of explanation are also found in Kneale (1949), and Friedman (1974). Cummins' (1983) view of explanation, especially what he calls 'system analysis,' is similar in several respects.

5. One simplification in particular worries me. The speaker's knowledge of the hearer's knowledge is an important ingredient in communication generally, but I have not included such knowledge in my models except for one type of indexical reference. Only in this case did such knowledge seem foundational for reference, even though it plays auxiliary

149

roles in other types of reference, and indeed, in all communication. Bach (1987) assigns a larger role to mutual knowledge.

6. For instance, Davidson (1984: xiii, 24, 30), Dowty, Peters, and Wall (1981: 2, 10), and Lycan (1984: 8–9) talk of their theories as explanatory, even though the main focus of their theories is specificatory.

7. Cropper (1970) describes this case.

8. My source here is Kuhn (1957: 142–144).

9. The interplay of specificatory and explanatory features in the development of science appears in recent discussions of superconductivity and of energy from nuclear fusion in beakers.

10. This has not always been the case. The traditional referential and ideational theories, as well as the stimulus-response theory, all aimed at being explanatory, that is, giving underlying conditions and mechanisms that constitute meaning. Wittgenstein's talk about language games, and Grice's theories of meaning and of implicatures also attempt to give conditions underlying phenomena, and thus are (partially) explanatory.

11. I use the term 'paradigm' here to mean methodology plus assumptions of content. I take it that this notion of paradigm resembles Kuhn's (1970), but nothing in my arguments hangs on this.

12. However, explanatory theories of reference do have implications for the semantics of sentences; such implications are discussed in several chapters, but especially chapter 7. Strong objections have been raised against truth-conditional semantics for sentences by authors in various disciplines (e.g., Atlas (1989), Lakoff (1987), and Winograd (1985)). These objections, in my opinion, mainly affect explanatory theories of language, and leave open the possibility of valuable specificatory use of truth-conditional semantics, especially in artificial intelligence (e.g., Sowa (1984) and Shapiro and Rapaport (1987)).

13. Quine uses the method of translation in his theorizing about language, and it leads him to conclude all of our theories about meaning are relative to an underlying presupposed language, and that we can never get rid of this relativity. It looks to me as though this relativity necessarily follows from the use of translation as the basic device of theorizing about language: translation always requires a target language into which the translation is made. Romanos' (1983: 91–98) excellent summary of Quine's main theories makes it clear that Quine concludes to the indeterminacy of translation because he uses translation as his basic theoretical device for studying language.

14. Though predication is a mechanism, stipulation is the absence of any mechanism, and is often used in the predicate-logic paradigm to specify reference (e.g., Lewis (1972)). Using stipulation is perfectly legitimate for specificatory, but not explanatory, theories of reference.

15. Wittgenstein (1953), Searle (1958), and Strawson (1959) had at earlier times pointed out problems in the description theory of proper names, but the latter two retained enough of that theory to be subject to Kripke's objections. The *persistence* of the description theory, not only in Strawson's and Searle's work, but in much philosophy after Kripke's criticisms, gives me pause. Could some a priori assumption account for it?

16. Not all philosophers working within the predicate-logic paradigm hold these assumptions. Cresswell (1973), Bach (1987), and Kaplan (1989a) hold that the pragmatics of indexicals is a part of semantics. Bach (1987), and Barwise and Perry (1983) hold that communication is important for data about reference.

17. For most of this paragraph I am indebted to Eileen Way.

18. Cf. Perry (1979, 1988) and Wettstein (1986, 1988). A related theory, also based on the sparseness of content in semantics, is McGinn's (1982) dichotomy between two kinds of linguistic meaning, truth-conditional content and conceptual role content. Like Perry and Wettstein, McGinn also has no theory of how these two are related. I discuss Perry's separation of semantics and pragmatics in my (forthcoming).

19. Two exceptions to this are Burge (1974) and Kamp (1990). Russell's account of indexicals and the reaction to it in the predicate-logic tradition corroborates some claims just made about perception and reference in that tradition. Russell had a perceptual theory for indexical reference, which called for immediate acquaintance with the object of perception. He did not articulate any structure within such perceptual reference, and instead treated the indexicals 'this' and 'that' as 'logically proper names' whose meaning was the referent. I suggest that one reason why he gave no articulate structure for perceptually based reference was that predicate-logic had no way of representing it. Followers of Russell did not like his theory of logically proper names, and dropped it. In doing so, they also dropped his perceptual theory of indexical reference, even though the latter theory had empirical features in its favor (cf. my 1984a). His followers could have dropped logically proper names and kept the perceptual theory of indexicals by developing a theory of the structures involved in perceptual indexical reference, but they did not. Why not?

20. A specificatory theory of reference might seem to be easier than an explanatory theory to transpose into a theory of necessary and sufficient truth conditions for reference, but one would still need to deal with initial conditions with a precision that specificatory theories do not guarantee.

21. Cf. my (1986a: 481) for another example of the separation of scientific models from necessary and sufficient conditions.

22. The notion of necessary and sufficient conditions is somewhat confusing because such conditions may be constitutive of a phenomenon,

or causes or effects of it, or logically equivalent to it; also they may be conditions of the existence of a phenomenon or for the truth of a sentence. In the sciences, one seeks conditions which constitute or cause a phenomenon, whereas in the predicate-logic paradigm, one seeks conditions expressed in predicate-logic that are materially or logically equivalent to a natural language sentence. The latter types of necessity and sufficiency indicate (at most) the equivalence needed for a correct translation, rather than a precise recipe for the existence of a phenomenon, as would be given by necessary and sufficient conditions in the sciences. The difference between the two types of necessary and sufficient conditions is vast. To figure out the scientific variety of necessary and sufficient conditions requires precise applications of the models to initial conditions, which requires detailed knowledge about both the initial conditions and the models. To state necessary and sufficient conditions of the scientific type for a candle flame takes several pages by Walker (1978) in *Scientific American*, whereas to state necessary and sufficient truth conditions for "The candle is lit" requires only a translation. However, to provide necessary and sufficient conditions of the scientific variety for linguistic phenomena involved in a use of the English sentence "The candle is lit" would be a mammoth undertaking.

23. Because Evans' (1982) approach to reference begins with the reference of thought, it is not surprising that an a priori principle (he calls it "Russell's principle") plays a major role in his theories.

24. The history of science supports this: consider Newton's invention of the calculus or Max Born's application of matrix theory to quantum mechanics (on the latter, see Cropper (1970: 89–90).

25. Rom Harré (1987, especially chapters 4 through 6) has given a fundamental role in his defense of realism in science to parts of my attention-directing model for reference.

Chapter 2: Indexicals and Two Models

1. I include demonstratives (e.g., 'this' or 'there') as indexicals because the same explanatory model covers them; this sameness will become apparent later. Cf. also endnote 12 below, and my (1992c).

2. In a different context, (1) could make a different type of reference, for example, suppose that the speaker is a tour-guide lecturer, who is showing people around a farm for raising and training guard dogs. He has been lecturing on the traits of various types of dog; in the context in which he uses (1), his reference is to the *breed* of dog, rather than to the individual dog *qua* particular. This is a version of what linguists call 'generic reference.' I am postponing to another time any discussion of generic reference, along with the associated topic of predication. The possibility of a generic interpretation of (1) was suggested to me by Roy Harris.

3. The fact that the explanations offered in the next three chapters provide no way to replace the word 'reference' indicates that only a partial explanation of reference is being attempted. In chapters 5 and 6, features of reference in addition to its determination are studied.

4. This is in contrast to Gareth Evans (1982), who takes indexical thought as foundational in his theory of indexicals. Since I view language as social, I take the hearer's determination of reference as a better starting point. Another reason why I focus on the hearer's discerning of indexical reference and not on the speaker's indexical thought is that the speaker chooses indexical phrases *opportunistically*, making use of what the context has to offer, so that indexical phrases often do not reflect how the speaker usually thinks of the referent.

5. The issue of tacit knowledge is important for Chomsky, and is connected with his doctrine of innate ideas; cf. Chomsky (1965) and especially Chomsky (1975) for his defense of tacit knowledge. For a review of some of the literature in the debate, and criticisms of tacit knowledge, cf. Raymond Nelson (1978) and Philip Kitcher (1978).

6. I am unwilling to call the view that indexicals function in virtue of the unique fit of descriptions a "descriptional" view of indexicals, because this terminological concession is reasonable only if one also makes the doctrinal concession that the only function of descriptions if that of being predicates. Since I am unwilling to make this doctrinal concession, I use the term 'predication' rather than 'descriptional.' Moreover, to use the phrase 'predication model' for the view that indexicals function in virtue of the fit of descriptions is more precise than to call it descriptional because 'predication model' catches the *role* (that of being uniquely fitting predicates) that descriptions play rather than the mere presence of descriptions.

7. Many other philosophers use versions of the predication model for indexicals, for example, Kaplan (1978, 1989a), Burge (1974), Brinton (1977), Weinstein (1974), Taylor (1980), and Evans (1982). Although Kaplan (1978: 233) suggests that descriptions in indexical phrases should be assimilated to pointing, he does not carry through on this suggestion, and does not offer any theory of how demonstration works in demonstrative reference. Kaplan clearly uses the predication model for indexicals in his examples, e.g., for the demonstrative use of 'the spy' he asks us to suppose "what is surely false" (1978: 234) that "there is one and only one spy"; a parallel supposition is made for 'dthat first child born in the twenty-first century' (1978: 241).

Burge (1974) and Brinton (1977) also use versions of the predication model, according to which descriptions in indexical REs are true (*but not uniquely true*) of their referents. Although Burge (1974: 212) says that the semantic interpretation of sentences containing indexical REs is completed extralinguistically, he (1974: 211) still takes descriptions in indexical REs to function in virtue of being true of the referent. In discussions of epistemic features associated with the use of indexicals, Burge (1977) emphasizes perception and memory rather than the fit of descriptions, but these epistemic views do not lead Burge to a theory of how indexical reference is determined, though he does recommend as a topic for research a perceptual paradigm for the relation between thinker and objects. Nor does Burge consider how a perceptual paradigm might relate to his earlier logical analysis of indexicals in which descriptions in indexical REs were taken to function in virtue of being true of the referent.

8. Cf. my (1984a) for a critical discussion of Russell's model and references to his work on it. Like Russell, Hector-Neri Castañeda (1980: 770) and David Woodruff Smith (1982: 181) also use the *speaker's* perception as determinative of indexical reference.

9. Russell and Reichenbach took indexical reference to be based on factors other than the particular use of an indexical. I (1984a) have argued that neither Russell's basis in egocentricity nor Reichenbach's basis in token-reflexivity is adequate as a general basis for determining indexical reference.

10. Three types of context can be grounds containing the referent: the physical surroundings, the discourse-dependent context, and the concerns of the conversers. To simplify the introduction of the model, I treat only the physical surroundings here, and take up the other two in the next chapter. Another simplification here is to limit the examples to cases in which the referent is a physical object; other types of referent are treated at beginning of the next chapter.

11. The context and the gestures which partition it are important not only for determining indexical reference but also as affecting the content expressed by indexical propositions, as will be seen in chapter 7.

12. I (1992c) have argued that Kaplan's (1989a) distinction between pure indexicals like 'now' and true demonstratives like 'this dog' does not concern their fundamental functioning. Instead, the very sounding of 'now' provides adequate perceptual clues to the location of the intended referent in the background, whereas a use of 'that dog' does not if there are several dogs around, so that gestures are needed.

13. This is Aristotle's phrase for a term which has one central meaning and several distinct meanings related to the central one.

14. "Figure-ground differentiation probably characterizes all perceptual experience" (Krech, David, Crutchfield, R.S., and Livson, N. (1969: 154)). Similar claims appear in most introductory psychology books.

15. In drawing a contrast to the predication model for reference, the figure-ground model for indexicals is parallel to the causal chain model for proper names. The latter, however, has substantially less positive content than the figure-ground model.

16. John Moulton and I deal with these details in an artificial intelligence (AI, for short) system for the figure-ground model. Our AI system aims at modeling the figure-ground model so as to provide more precise descriptions of contexts, gestures, figures, and their functioning. In particular, we modify a semantic network device so that it includes information about context and gestures as well as about descriptions, and we have the semantic network send the information about context, gestures, and figures to a connectionist device, which scans a simulated context for the referent. It if picks out a referent, information about it is sent back to the semantic network device. Further description of our AI model is in Moulton and Roberts (1991, 1992).

17. This example was suggested to me by Peter Strawson. Bach (1987: 191) gives a number of similar examples.

18. A critic has suggested that some predicate must be true of the referent in the case of (7) and (8); this suggestion is correct, but holds for anything in the universe. My point about the predicates of (7) and (8) is that they may function not only as predicates, but also as complements to indexicals; that is, they function in virtue of providing a figure that is to enable the hearer to pick out the referent, whether or not the predicate is true of the referent.

19. Colin McGinn (1981) takes the spatio-temporal location of the referent of an indexical to be essential to the determination of its reference. His view is discussed in the Polemics section of chapter 3.

20. Exceptions to this point are taken up at the beginning of the next chapter.

21. Whether the description so obtained functions within the proposition or outside of the proposition at the pragmatic level will not be discussed now, since the objections to be raised in this section against these expanded descriptions affect both cases.

22. Though picking out the speaker of (15) visually would usually be required for the hearer to discern the referent of 'I' in (15), sight is not the only sense that can be used in picking a thing out of its background. If the hearer already knew the sound of the speaker's voice, then he might have been able to pick out the speaker from the background on that basis. Or if the hearer was blind, and had become very skilled at discerning voices, he might be able to identify a person just as well as a sighted person, but do so by hearing rather than sight. In either of these cases, the hearer of (15) could pick the speaker out of the background despite failure to see the speaker.

23. John Searle (1979: 145) has suggested such a replacement in cases of referentially used descriptions, which, I argue in chapter 4, are a variety of indexical RE. I do not use Searle's example because it has the

hearer's attention already focused on the referent, and thus provides a poor test for whether the predication model serves to focus the hearer's attention on a referent.

24. There is evidence from experimental psychology for the point that people use descriptions at a perceptual level in guiding searches, as contrasted to some higher cognitive level. Ulric Neisser (1964 in 1971) reports experiments showing exactly this point. I wish to thank Eileen Way for calling Neisser's article to my attention.

25. Examples like (19) show an inconsistency in Alan Brinton's (1977) doctrine of indexicals. He holds that indexicals of the form 'that F' function partly in virtue of F's being true of the referent, but he holds that in sentences of the form 'that is F' the predicate contributes to the determination of the reference of the indexical by some unspecified means other than that of being true of the referent. One might well question why this unspecified means is not operative also in the case of 'that F.'

26. Donnellan (1966 in 1977: 56, note 9) makes this argument for referentially used descriptions.

27. In using the topic-comment distinction for explaining the truth-value assignments for propositions in which indexicals lack a referent, I am obviously indebted to Peter Strawson (1964). The topic-comment distinction is motivated quite independently of issues concerning indexical reference; cf. John Lyons (1977b: 500–511) and Charles Li and Sandra Thompson (1976).

28. Both the usual implication of the existence of a referent when one uses an indexical, and the absence of such an implication in the present example, can be explained by a theory of the conditions under which the use of an indexical implies the existence of a referent for it. Martinich (1984: ch. 9) views such implications as matters of Gricean implicature. However, this usual implication may be missing when the indexical is part of a negated clause as in (27). More on reference and existence is in chapter 7.

29. Cf. my (1984a); since rigidity concerns reference rather than meaning, and since reference is a matter of the use of expressions and not just of their meaning, rigidity must also be a matter of use. My view of rigidity is closer to Kaplan's (1989a) than to Kripke's.

30. This restriction has been suggested by Plantinga (1978), Kaplan (1989a), and others.

31. The RE 'the actual world' must function on something other than the predication model because no human knows a description (not based on indexicals or proper names) that fits only the actual world and not some other possible world as well (consider that in some possible world other than the actual world the number of leaves on all the trees in the world is

one more than that in the actual world). The example of the leaves, but not its use, is from Peter van Inwagen (1980).

32. The world in which an indexical is used is usually the actual world. However, fictional characters may use indexicals in relation to the possible world created by the fiction. Nevertheless, for brevity, I will speak of the actual world, rather than of the world in which an indexical is used.

33. Kripke (1971 in 1977) holds that the reidentification of referents of rigid designators is a pseudo-problem, but he says that the referent is fixed by *stipulation*. This use of stipulation was objected to by Saarinen (1982). The figure-ground model replaces this stipulation by the functioning of a figure in relation to a ground in one possible world only.

34. Salmon (1981) calls a rigid designator which refers to the same referent in all possible worlds, including those in which it does not exist, an 'obstinate' rigid designator.

35. My talk about possible worlds bothers some otherwise sympathetic readers, because they view such talk as requiring some *semantic* or *metaphysical* theory of possible worlds, precisely the kind of theory that one wants to avoid in a naturalistic approach to reference. But I do not use the phrase, 'possible worlds,' to refer to entities in semantic or metaphysical explanations. Thus, my use differs markedly from uses of possible worlds to explain propositional attitudes, the connection of sense and reference, or counterfactuals. (Cf. Lycan (1979: 274–275, 310) for a discussion of various uses of possible worlds.) I view possible worlds as ad hoc abstract entities (rather like Ptolemaic epicycles) with a useful role in logic, but no role at all in semantics or metaphysics. I view logic in general as a specificatory device with the practical purpose of checking on validity, but with no explanatory function in semantics or metaphysics. (Cf. chapter 7 and endnote 15 there on the practical nature of logic.) In regard to reference, there is no semantic or metaphysical role for possible worlds in explaining the determination of reference on either the figure-ground or predication models. On the figure-ground model, reference is determined in relation to the context of use, so that the referent is picked out of the actual world context only. On the predication model, a description refers to whatever is F, and not to a certain individual *qua* individual. I view talk about picking the referent out of alternative possible worlds on the predication model as a manner of speaking, whose cash value is simply that a description 'whatever is F' is likely to fit different individuals in alternative possible circumstances. But this point is a truism about descriptions and alternative possible circumstances, and requires no supposition that alternative possible worlds exist as explanatory entities.

36. I would like to thank the students in my seminar in philosophy of language at Binghamton University in the spring of 1992, especially Jonathan Beskin and Philip Gross, for helpful comments on this chapter.

Chapter 3: The Figure-Ground Model: Varieties of Context

1. This use of the presence of a part of a thing can handle problems about indexical reference to very large things, whether perceivable or not, as long as a part of them is present in the surroundings, for example, 'this country' or 'this continent.'

2. Somewhat similar to (2) are what Evans (1982: 145), following Quine (1968 in 1969: 40–41), calls "deferred ostension," and Bach (1987: 193) calls "descriptive reference by means of indexicals." Evans' example is:

i. That man is going to be sorry.

(i) is said while pointing to a car with traffic tickets on it. If (i) is to express an indexical reference, (i) would preferably be stated, on my model, by

ii. That car owner is going to be sorry.

However, I find (ii) unclear, since car owners are not as closely connected with their cars as authors are with their books (e.g., the author is the main cause of the book, and her name is prominently placed on the book, and the book *qua* type is permanently hers). The point of (i) is better made by

iii. Whoever is the owner of that car is going to be sorry.

This interpretation of what is going on in (i) brings in the distinction from the next chapter between referential and attributive uses of REs. In (i), 'that man' is viewed as attributively used because it is a sloppily expressed shorter form of (iii). Whether 'that man' is referentially or attributively used in (i) can be diagnosed only in a larger context, in which it becomes clear whether the referent is spoken about *qua* particular or *qua* member of a kind. Examples in which indexicals are used in an attributive way are not surprising since the definite article 'the' is demonstrative in its origins, and gives rise to attributively used definite descriptions. In the next chapter in endnote 10, I suggest how 'the' comes to have a role in attributively used descriptions.

3. That a discourse context contains a referent by expressing it explicitly has nothing to do with the direct reference theory, which states that the referent itself is in propositions. Rather, explicit containment in discourse is a matter of explicitly directing attention within discourse to the referent.

4. My arguments for this are in the next chapter, where I argue that referentially used descriptions function on the figure-ground model.

5. This example was suggested to me by Peter Strawson.

6. Not all reference by means of indexicals to things as contained in the discourse-dependent context is to be explained by the figure-ground model. Some varieties of such reference require the predication model for

an account of the determination of their reference. However, in the present discussion I will treat only cases where the figure-ground model is required.

7. Note that the discourse-dependent context can supply both figure and ground in the same sentence.

8. John Lyons (1977: 667–669) extends the use of the term 'anaphora' to cover cases of indexical reference on the basis of things presupposed but not explicitly referred to in the context (as in the case of 'she' (12)), but he assigns a non-anaphorical status to indexical reference on the basis of the physical presence of symbols in the discourse (as made by 'that term' in (13)) or on the basis of an earlier statement of fact in the discourse (as in the case of 'that' in (9) and (10)).

9. The mother and father are causes of the baby, but this is not the basis of the reference; even if the baby were adopted, the reference would work in the same way.

10. "Concerns" is an ambiguous term: it may mean either a certain kind of psychological state or an object of such a state. The latter meaning is employed here: on my view, the second kind of discourse-independent context is the set of objects of certain kinds of psychological states of the conversers.

11. In discussions, Jay Atlas raised the question of why indexical reference based on the presence of a thing in the concerns of the conversers normally uses 'the' rather than 'this' or 'that.' The likely reason is the same as for anaphorical reference: the referent is already closely connected with the attention of the conversers.

12. Rom Harré has suggested to me that the hearer of (15) might discern the referent of 'the new car' in (15) even if the use of (15) was the first that he had heard of the car. I think this is correct, but two qualifications are needed in this suggestion: first, the hearer would have to know that the speaker sometimes owns cars, and second, a question about the identity of the car would be much more likely in Harré's case than in the case in which the hearer antecedently knew about the new car.

13. I discuss the structures involved in visual perception of the physical surroundings because these are usually important for indexical reference based on physical surroundings; structures, however, are also present in the physical surroundings as perceived by hearing or smell or touch.

14. Gibson's views on affordances that are reported here are from his seminar at SUNY Binghamton on February 24, 1976. His views about the importance of structures in the environment for perception are still prominent in psychology; for example, a recent paper by Whitman Richards (1992) focused on the role of structures within visual phenomena for vision.

15. Ruth Garrett Millikan (1984) has interesting things to say about indexical reference, especially in regard to a metaphysical scheme within which she locates such reference. She takes indexical reference to be a device established by natural selection, with the result that it has proper functions determining how it works. This general metaphysical picture is quite compatible with the figure-ground model. The details that she offers for the functioning of indexicals, however, do not seem to me to fit together into a coherent theory. At times, she describes indexical reference as perceptual and based on our tracking abilities (1984: 172–173) and as social, involving the directing of the hearer's attention (1984: 165). At other times, however, she takes indexical reference to depend upon true description (1984: 171) rather than perception, and she assigns what appears *prima facie* to be an individualistic nature to the identification of the referent of an indexical: she (1984: 162) says that identifying the referent of an indexical is translating the indexical into an inner name for the referent. This notion of an inner name is to be replaced later by her theory of acts of identification, but it is not clear to me how this is to be done.

16. Cf. my (1993) for criticisms of Kaplan's arguments.

17. McGinn's account, in my opinion, takes a step in the right direction by providing rules for the *hearer*, rather than the speaker, to use in discerning the referent of an indexical (e.g., 1981: 164–165, 167).

Chapter 4: The Referential-Attributive Distinction

1. Donnellan's 1966 essay and its examples were formative in my thinking about reference.

2. Kripke (1977: 262) also comments on this point.

3. This example of Donnellan's also shows that the determination of the status of descriptions as referential or attributive within a sentence may not be possible if only the sentence containing them is considered; the discourse outside of that sentence may also have to be considered.

4. I prefer to speak about reference to a member of a kind rather than about reference to a member of a set because sets might be picked out by enumeration of the individuals that are their members, whereas it is the property or properties expressed by attributively used descriptions which pick out the referents. However, because I am using the word 'kind' merely to make the point that the referent is picked out by the properties, I use 'kind' in a very general way so that it includes events and deficiencies, as well as what would ordinarily be called kinds.

5. I call these models 'semantic' for short, even though they are also pragmatic in that they involve contexts. Note that these are not models of Gricean pragmatics because they affect the contributions from definite descriptions to propositions (or to 'what is said' in Grice's (1975) sense).

6. The application of the figure-ground model to referentially used descriptions has important results for the presupposition of the existence of the referent, which will be discussed in chapter 7.

7. There could be a courtroom context in which 'the murderer of Smith' is used referentially, and then (8) would be validly derived from (1 DC).

8. This point about descriptions contained in comments is from Strawson (1964).

9. Cf. my (1984b) and (1987) on ambiguity.

10. A question still remains as to how 'the' manages to be involved in such diverse constructions. In its origins, 'the' is a demonstrative; thus, there seems to be no problem in its use in DC. But how can it have come to be employed in the IP construction, since an indefinite pronoun seems far removed from a demonstrative? My answer to this question is that IP may be viewed as closely related to an anaphorical use of a demonstrative in which a demonstrative is in apposition with an indefinite RE of the form 'whatever is the one and only F." Thus, the underlying form for (1 IP) would be

1 IP'. That one, whoever is the one and only murderer of Smith, is insane.

Some support for viewing IP as closely related to such a construction may be found in the fact that propositions containing attributively used descriptions are easily converted to conjunctions of two propositions, of which one has an indefinite RE as its subject, and the other has a demonstrative coreferential with that RE, for example:

1 IP''. Some (and only one) person murdered Smith; that person is insane.

The fundamental references in (1 IP') by 'whoever is the one and only murderer of Smith' and in (1 IP'') by 'some person' involve non-rigid designation; since the demonstratives in these two sentences are coreferential with these REs, they are also non-rigid. This non-rigidity appears also in the attributive use of a definite description, which I take to be closely related to the constructions in (1 IP') and (1 IP'').

If it is correct to view 'the' in IP as closely related to an anaphorical use of a demonstrative, then there is an easy answer to the original question of whether there is lexical ambiguity of 'the' in DC and IP uses: 'the' is not ambiguous in these two constructions because it has the same basic demonstrative function in both. What differs between the two constructions is the *syntactic and semantic functioning of descriptions*. Whether a demonstrative has an anaphorical or non-anaphorical function, or whether it appears in an abbreviated construction (like IP) or in unabbreviated constructions as in (1 IP') or (1 IP''), it retains the same meaning. Therefore, there is no reason to invoke lexical ambiguity of 'the' in explaining the referential-attributive distinction. (I would like to thank John Lyons for encouragement in this line of speculation about 'the,' and for comments on an earlier version of this chapter; his (1975) paper was also very helpful to me.) Only after I figured out this account of how 'the' could be used attributively did it strike me that what Evans and Quine call 'deferred ostension,' and what Bach calls 'descriptive reference with indexicals' are additional cases of attributive uses of demonstratives; for references on this, cf. footnote 2 of chapter 3.

11. Dennis W. Stampe (1974: 189–192) has noted this point.

12. Since many authors have taken the referential-attributive distinction to be semantic, the popularity of Gricean pragmatic interpretations of it is surprising. Among those who take the distinction to be semantic are not only Donnellan (1978), but also Stalnaker (1972), Burge (1974), Stampe (1974), Brinton (1977), Kaplan (1978), Peacocke (1975), Wilson (1978), and Devitt (1981)). I read a version of the following discussion of Kripke's views at the Eastern Division meeting of the American Philosophical Association in 1978.

13. Searle (1979: 154, 157) is aware of such counter-examples, but views them as casting doubt on the referential-attributive distinction in general rather than on his interpretation of it. The counter-examples, however, directly hit his version of the distinction. Such examples, including (22), have no adverse effect on my interpretation of the distinction.

14. I learned of Dennis W. Stampe's (1974) paper on the referential-attributive distinction when I was in the final stages of copyediting this book. He argues for a semantic status for the distinction, and focuses mainly on attributive uses. His discussion, in my opinion, is the most interesting one in the literature on attributive uses. Stampe bases his analysis on a distinction between *subject-wanting* and *predicate-wanting* questions. The latter aim at learning something about an already identified individual, for example:

i. Who is that man, who is the man who murdered Smith?

Stampe (1974: 166) suggests this context for (i): it is asked "after we've nabbed the murderer, but find him to be a stranger who carries no identification." Consider, in contrast, a subject-wanting question:

ii. Who murdered Smith?

In this case, according to Stampe (1974: 166), "the inquirer himself supplies the predicate he is concerned with ('murdered Smith') and what he *wants* is the subject to which it may be ascribed." Stampe views attributive uses as deriving from subject-wanting questions in this way: attributive uses of 'the F' express the irrelevance to 'the F is G' of an answer to the subject-wanting question 'Who is the F?'. Because of this irrelevance, Stampe (1974: 171, 193) views attributive uses as expressing (but not stating) a relation between being F and being G. Clearly Stampe (1974: 171) assigns a predicative functioning to attributive uses of 'the F', and to this extent concurs with my views. However, his analysis is somewhat more complicated than mine in two ways: he prefers the phrasing 'whoever it may be who is the F', and he locates this clause not among the usual constituents of a sentence, but at a higher level, in the speech act clause. I do not think his argument for the latter of these two features is successful, but I cannot discuss it here. However, I view his (1974: 173–179) *syntactically* based arguments for treating 'the F' used attributively as a predicate in a 'whoever'-clause as a welcome addition to the *semantic* support given for my account of attributive uses.

I wish to thank Gerald Vision for pointing out Stampe's paper to me.

15. There are other construals of the referential-attributive distinction that are of some interest, but which fail for various reasons: for example, those offered by Stalnaker (1972) and Bell (1973). I omit discussion of these accounts because of lack of space.

Chapter 5: Specific and Non-Specific Reference

1. Philosophers (e.g., Kamp (1984), Heim (1983)) who work in discourse representation semantics have noted the distinction; their focus on discourse as a whole is valuable, but they have dropped the question of how REs relate to things outside of discourse. This question may be put aside for certain purposes in representing language, but it remains an interesting question for one who wishes to understand how reference works.

2. Geach (1962) has also argued that indefinite descriptions do not refer at all. One problem in this argument is that there is no generally accepted theory of reference on the basis of which he can exclude indefinite descriptions from reference. A reader raised the following Geachean objection to taking indefinite descriptions as referring: if 'I met a man' is false because I met no one, what does 'a man' refer to? My reply is that on my view, reference does not require the existence of the referent: the account of reference that is developed in chapter 6 takes reference to be constituted by a certain type of attention-directing, rather than by a relation to an existing referent. This attention-directing can occur in the absence of a referent, and this holds not only for reference by means of indefinite descriptions, but also for reference by means of indexicals and definite descriptions. In the proposed counterexample, 'a man' directs attention to a thing *qua* member of a kind, 'man,' if the RE is used to make non-specific reference. If it is used to make specific reference, then 'a man' directs attention to a thing *qua* particular that is identified for the audience as a member of the kind, 'man.'

3. Strawson in *Individuals* speaks of both introduction and identification, but says that term introduction "essentially involves the idea of iden-

tification" (1959 in 1963: 184), and in another place he uses the two notions as equivalent ("introduce, i.e., identify" (1959 in 1963: 222). However, Strawson is clearly talking about identification *simpliciter*, rather than about *identification for the audience*, so that his view is not explicitly opposed to mine; rather my distinction between introduction of the referent and its identification for the audience can be taken as a development on his views. The only precedent I could find for my distinction between introduction and identification for the audience was in George Wilson (1978: 74); he distinguished indicating one's intention to ascribe a property to an object from identifying the relevant object. Though this distinction is rather like mine, I disagree with several other main points in his paper.

4. I realize that 'talking about a thing' does not require reference (cf. Bach (1987: 49–50)), but reference is an important means for talking about individuals. Additional features of reference, beyond talking about a thing, will be developed in this chapter and the next.

5. This example is from Isard (1975: 291).

6. Let me review some tricky terminology here. Reference *qua* particular concerns the manner of referring to a thing, and occurs in indexical reference, in referential uses of definite descriptions, and in the introduction of a thing into a proposition by an indefinite description used to make specific reference. Reference to a unique F occurs in attributively used descriptions, even though such reference is not *qua* particular. Reference to a single thing may occur not only in all the types of reference just mentioned, but also in non-specific reference made by means of a description of the form 'an F.' In this last case, it is left indeterminate which individual is this single thing, and a set of individuals may be matched one for one with another set in discourse, as in (18) below.

7. I had originally thought that the coreference of 'she,' a rigid designator in the 'if'-clause of (13), with 'a certain very intelligent woman' showed that the latter was a rigid designator, but my study of Evans' E-type anaphora (cf. chapters 3 and 7) and related cases showed me that this was not a valid form of argument. Note also that 'she' might be coreferential with a non-rigid description, for example:

i. John wants to marry an intelligent woman; she should also inherit a fortune. But he won't decide whom to propose to for at least five years.

[This example is from a reader.] The coreferentiality of 'she' in (i) with a non-rigid designator is shown by the fact that in alternative possible worlds, different individuals would satisfy the description.

8. Strawson (1950 in 1963: 190) held that indefinite descriptions differ from definite ones in regard to identifying the referent for the audience, and that secrecy might motivate such withholding of identification.

9. The principle of identification requires that a speaker be able to identify a referent in order to refer to it. A version of the principle plays a

major role in Evans' (1982) book, where it is called 'Russell's Principle.' Similar principles appear in Russell (1912: 58), Strawson (1959 in 1963: 184–190), and Donnellan (1978), and a weaker version of it appears as far back as John Locke (1959 ed., vol. 2, p. 9). The principle of identification has various forms depending upon (a) whether the identification is for the reference of REs or of thoughts, (b) whether the means of identification is by the predication model or by perception, and (c) whether the identification is to be based on the individual speaker alone or on society. If one emphasizes the truth of descriptions, a very intellectualist view of language emerges; this can be avoided by allowing perceptions also to play an important role in identification. If one's study begins with the reference of thought, the result need not be intellectualist (e.g., Evans begins with thought but does not neglect perception), but the result is likely to be an individualistic rather than societal view of identification: it seems impossible to identify something within one's thought without having some identifying description or perception of it. In contrast, if one begins the study of reference with a study of communication, one is more open to the social determinants of reference, which may allow someone else's thoughts and practices to identify the referent. Clearly, such determination by other people is needed for (16 A).

10. Societal cooperation in determining reference is not limited to introducing a referent *qua* particular and identifying the referent *qua* member of a kind for the audience. Societal cooperation might also underlie identifying the referent *qua* particular. This is done in the case of certain descriptions (e.g., 'the prime meridian') and proper names. These topics go beyond what can be included in this book.

11. The specific-non-specific distinction is not epistemic, since specific reference can occur when the speaker has knowledge sufficient to identify the referent, as in (14) and (15), and when he lacks such knowledge, as in (16 A). Therefore, an account like that of Jackendoff (1972), which attempts to explain specific reference by means of the speaker's epistemic state, will not work.

12. Barbara Hall Partee (1970: 362) makes this objection.

Chapter 6: Attention-Directing Models for the Basic Nature of Reference

1. My procedure in the next chapter will be to set aside speech act theory, and to say a little about the functioning of subject-predicate contexts as well as a variety of contexts where the relating function relates more than the object of the specificatory functioning to other things in discourse. This procedure yields only very rough models of certain features which affect the relating function in propositional contexts, but not an explanatory model for propositions in general.

2. I do not know whether there are more kinds of non-propositional settings for reference.

3. Note that attention is directed to the attitude and feelings of the speaker by means both of the meaning of 'idiot' and of the presence of an emotional tone in the way that 'That idiot' is said.

4. Another problem for the direct reference theory concerns contexts involving existence, identity, or propositional attitudes. In the next chapter, I will argue that the attention-directing models lead to explanations of such contexts that are better than those of any extensional view of reference, including the direct reference theory.

5. Perry (1980) does this, as does Wettstein (1986). Stalnaker (1987) makes a similar move.

6. Further reasons for distinguishing specification of the referent from relating it to other things in a proposition will appear in discussions of opacity in modal and attitudinal contexts in the next chapter.

7. The examples are from Ochs and Schieffelin (1983: 158, 161).

8. This is not the only use of left dislocation: cf. Ochs and Schieffelin (1983: 111). In addition, a referee suggested that left-dislocation may also occur in planned discourse, for example, 'As for Smith's second argument, I shall postpone discussion of it for a while.'

9. Cf. Ochs and Schieffelin (1983: 67).

10. Though advocates of possible worlds semantics talk of functions from REs or descriptive terms to extensions across possible worlds, these functions are specified by stipulations and circular devices (e.g., 'dog' is a function from possible worlds to dogs). In commenting on possible worlds semantics, Janet Fodor (1977: 41) says that it "does not offer full specifications of the intensions of particular lexical items, and hence does not in fact characterize the meanings of any sentences at all."

11. The distinction between achievements and activities is important in Aristotle (*Nicomachaean Ethics*, bk. 7) and Ryle (1949, 1954).

Chapter 7: Applications of the Models to Existence, Identity, and Opacity

1. Frege (1950, 1956) views senses as eternal, unchanging, and belonging to a third realm, distinguished from the physical world and from the mental world.

2. Note that the direct reference theory is not the only view that treats reference extensionally (as defined). In the possible worlds seman-

tics of Lewis (1972), for instance, lists containing stipulations of referents for proper names and indexicals are used, so that the referent itself is represented in the semantics without any account of the natural language means by which it is determined. Even though possible worlds semantics is called "intensional," I view it as extensional in regard to reference not based on predication because in treating such reference, it omits the means and includes only the extensions across possible worlds.

3. Related to this paradox about informativeness is the view of Ruth Barcan Marcus and Saul A. Kripke that identity statements whose REs are proper names or indexicals are necessarily true if true at all. William Kneale and Martha Kneale (1962: 604) view the necessity of identity statements as a paradox, though many philosophers now view it as nonparadoxical. Of course, in Barcan Marcus' (1947, 1961, 1962) logical system and in Kripke's (1971, 1980) logical system, identity statements involving proper names or indexicals are necessary. What is questionable, and perhaps a source of paradox, is the supposition that these logics exactly mirror identity statements in natural language. The present discussion, however, focuses mainly on the informativeness of identity statements. I discuss the necessity of identity statements elsewhere (1985, 1992a, 1992b).

4. This purpose for identity claims is especially important in the sciences, for example:

i. Temperature is identical with mean kinetic energy.

5. The exceptions who are on my side on this issue are Frege and Kearns. In his *Begriffsschrift*, Frege says ". . . that the *same content*, in a particular case, is actually given by *two modes of determination* is the content of a *judgement*" (1879: 14–15, as translated in Currie (1982: 100)). Later Frege (1892 in 1950) apparently rejected this view. Kearns' (1984: 451–453; cf. also 87–90, 442–443) analysis of identity statements is similar to mine, and has an added advantage of being a formal analysis.

6. When I say that existence claims are *about* ways of specifying reference, the aboutness is nothing but the point that the subject RE in an existence claim expresses a way of specifying reference *about which* it is asserted that it succeeds (or it is asserted that it doesn't succeed) in specifying a referent in the real world.

7. Janet Fodor (1979) pointed out that other logical operations also fail in opaque contexts.

8. Others (e.g., Achinstein (1979)) apparently have drawn the conclusion that reference does not occur inside opaque contexts. I once mistakenly thought that Linsky (1983: 102) drew this conclusion, but I now view this passage as indicating the views of others.

9. My attitude toward opacity and transparency in this paragraph is very different from Quine's. He (1961: 139) sometimes views the failure of

SUB as paradoxical, and he says that "one rightly expects substitutivity of identity in discourse about the identical object" (1961: 151). Quine explains opacity only partially. He aims less at understanding opacity than at segregating it. Towards this goal, he clarifies the extent of opacity in a variety of contexts, and he develops artificial notations for marking clearly whether a term occurs opaquely (for an example regarding attitudinal contexts, he (1960: 150) suggests 'believes x to have . . .' for transparent x, and 'believes that x . . .' for opaque x). He (1960: 216–221) also discusses the extent to which we can do without opaque contexts, arguing for the conclusion that we don't need them at all for a canonical notation for the sciences. I find this conclusion bizarre, if the canonical notation is to represent not only theories but also data. Opaque contexts are among the data of natural language, and I expect that at some distant time there will exist a science of natural language.

10. Philosophers have also argued against SUB (e.g., Linsky (1965) and Cartwright (1971)); Barcan Marcus (1975) argues in favor of SUB, but as a normative rather than descriptive principle. As such it sets ideals for analysis, but does not automatically licence natural language inferences.

11. This is not always the case, as shown by types (F, G, H, and I) of referential opacity below.

12. This account of how indexicals usually presuppose the existence of their referents is in the spirit of a suggestion by Levinson (1983: 225): "what we need is a theory that predicts presuppositions from the semantic specification of linguistic expressions."

13. I do not claim that topic-comment always coincides with subject-predicate, but only that it often does.

14. Quine (1960: 146) makes related points about the predicates 'refer' and 'is true.'

15. Earlier in the twentieth century, logic was viewed as an idealization (e.g., Hempel (1956)); a related view is Barcan Marcus' (1975) position that logic is normative.

16. I view contexts of propositional attitude as a subspecies of psychological contexts, all of which can produce opacity. Another subspecies is psychological contexts which lack explicit psychological verbs (e.g., 'John ran swiftly past the yard to avoid a vicious dog'). Yet another kind of psychological context is not propositional (e.g., 'I want a horse'). And there are contexts which compound propositional attitudes with other features so as to affect reference; cf. endnote 24.

17. Though I came to this view independently, it has already appeared in Dennett (1982), Searle (1979 in 1979), and Stich (1983).

18. As mentioned above, though one person may play both roles in a report, I am omitting such cases.

19. Speaker's reference here does not involve a contrast to semantic reference, as in Kripke's (1977) use of the phrase. Rather my point is that the speaker makes and vouches for the reference, as contrasted to his reporting how someone else makes a reference.

20. The presupposition of existence of the tree holds in (18), but there are other causes of the failure of EG besides using an RE within an attitudinal context not to make the speaker's reference, as we will see.

21. Note that the fact that an RE is used to report how the reportee specifies the referent does not entail that the RE is not used to make the speaker's reference. This second point is instead required by the attributive uses of descriptions because when they are inside an attitudinal context, they do not provide any mechanism for assigning responsibility for reference to the speaker.

22. Though the inference from (23) to (24) is valid, SUB as used in *Rule 2* is not a mere matter of substituting coreferential REs, since the REs involved are not coreferential by themselves. Rather, they are coreferential as parts of acts of referring which involve certain contexts, and perhaps also gestures. To view these two indexical phrases as simply coreferential omits their indexical status, and treats them as though the phrases in isolation from other factors were coreferential, which they are not.

23. Because ways of specifying reference are kinds of attention-directing, they are very finely distinguished. The mere fact that one's attention is directed to a thing in one way does not entail that it is also directed to that thing in any other way.

24. Attitudinal contexts can interact with any type of context, including other opaque and other attitudinal contexts. Perry's (1979) essential indexicals combine attitudinal contexts with explanations of behavior (cf. my (forthcoming)). Castaneda's (1966, 1967, 1968) quasi-indexicals are cases in which the speaker and reportee are identical; these amount to a combination of attitudinal contexts with reflexives (cf. my (1986b, 1988)), for example:

i.   John believes that he (himself) is rich.

ii. I believe that I am the editor of *Soul*.

25. This does not require the presence of the referent itself in propositions (i.e., the direct reference theory). Instead, attention is directed to the referent on the figure-ground model, and then that object of attention-directing is related to the property or relation expressed by the verb as in alternative possible circumstances.

26. A reader raised the question of my criterion for sameness of attribute. My answer is a version of Leibniz' law: two properties are identical if they have all properties in common. This can be shown either by a

scientific theory, which shows the identity of a surface-level property and an underlying property, for example, temperature and mean kinetic energy respectively (cf. Aronson (1984)), or by synonymy (for which I can offer only intuitions). My present purpose of providing linguistic accounts of attribute-identity contexts, however, is distinct from that of offering a theory of attribute-identity; the latter is a difficult metaphysical question.

27. Perhaps the reason why 'oculist' and 'ophthalmologist' contribute different ways of specifying reference concerns the words themselves; words are part of the way of specifying reference. If one were to rule out any verbal contribution, and require that the contribution be only at some more abstract level, then perhaps these two terms could be taken to express the same way of specifying reference. This kind of move may be needed for maintaining the view that propositions can be identical across languages. On the latter view, there must be some way to express the same proposition in two different languages. Then one could speak an amalgam of the two languages, and within this amalgam, rephrase the puzzle in (43) and (44). And one would have to allow that REs in each language may make the same contribution to proposition-identity claims if one holds that propositions can be the same across languages.

28. Urmson (1968) has noted the opacity of such contexts.

29. For instance, the model could be blown to bits at the instant that it is completed.

30. This rephrasing is only approximate because (58) does not explicitly say that doing something at dusk did *not* cause Socrates' death. Literally, the parallel clarifying the contrast in (58) would be:

58 A'. It was the drinking of hemlock that caused Socrates' death, and it is not said whether the fact that it was done at dusk was a cause.

However, in most contexts there is a conversational implicature from (58) to (58 A). It is also noteworthy that these paraphrases assimilate underlining for semantic emphasis to clauses beginning with 'the fact that.' But neither of these produce opacity by themselves; they do so only when interacting with another context whose truth conditions are affected by differences in the cause or fact clauses (e.g., identity or explanation contexts).

31. Geach (1962) first noticed the opacity produced by reflexives.

32. Note that the same modification of the predicate by a reflexive is present also in non-opaque contexts, even though it does not affect truth conditions in such contexts any differently than would a coreferential RE that was not reflexive—this point indicates another case in which there is more to meaning than truth conditions.

33. I wish to thank an anonymous reader for the suggestion of the correct quantified version of (60).

34. I would not be surprised if there are additional features of discourse which put REs to double use. I also suspect that there are yet more kinds of opacity based on the referential functioning.

Afterword

1. Putnam's argument for the indeterminacy of reference in model-theoretic semantics was already have mentioned in chapter 1. The connections of language to ideas and behavior are equally problematical for such semantics; cf. Partee (1979, 1980, 1982).

Bibliography

Achinstein, Peter. "The Causal Relation." *Midwest Studies in Philosophy* IV (1979) 369–386.

Almog, J., Perry, J., and Wettstein, H. (eds.). *Themes from Kaplan.* New York: Oxford Univ. Press, 1989.

Alston, William P. *Philosophy of Language.* Englewood Cliffs: Prentice-Hall, 1964.

Anderson, A. R., Marcus, R. B., and Martin, R. M. (eds.). *The Logical Enterprise.* New Haven: Yale University Press, 1975.

Anderson, C. A., and Owens, J. (eds.). *Propositional Attitudes.* Stanford: Center for the Study of Language and Information, 1990.

Aristotle. *Nicomachaean Ethics.* Translated by M. Ostwald. Indianapolis: Bobbs-Merrill, 1962.

Aronson, Jerrold L. *A Realist Philosophy of Science.* London: Macmillan, 1984.

Atlas, Jay David. *Philosophy Without Ambiguity.* Oxford: Clarendon Press, 1989.

Bach, Emmon. "Nouns and Noun Phrases." *Universals in Linguistic Theory.* Ed. by E. Bach and R. Harms. New York: Holt, Rinehart and Winston, 1968, 90–122.

Bach, E., and Harms, R. (eds.). *Universals in Linguistic Theory.* New York: Holt, Rinehart and Winston, 1968.

Bach, Kent. *Thought and Reference.* Oxford: Clarendon Press, 1987.

Baeuerle, R., Schwarze, C., and Stechow, A. von (eds.). *Meaning, Use, and Interpretation of Language.* Berlin: de Gruyter, 1983.

173

Bar-Hillel, Yehoshua. "Indexical Expressions." *Mind* 63 (1954) 359–379.

Barwise, Jon, and Perry, John. *Situations and Attitudes*. Cambridge: MIT Press, 1983.

Bell, J. M. "What is Referential Opacity?" *Journal of Philosophical Logic* 2 (1973) 155–180.

Berger, Alan, "A Theory of Reference Transmission and Reference Change." *Midwest Studies in Philosophy*. Ed. by P. French, T. E. Uehling, and H. K. Wettstein. Notre Dame: University of Notre Dame Press, 1989, 180–198.

Blackburn, Simon (ed.). *Meaning, Reference, and Necessity*. Cambridge: Cambridge Univ. Press, 1975.

Brinton, Alan. "Definite Descriptions and Context-Dependence." *Nous* 11 (1977) 397–407.

Brown, Roger. *Words and Things*. New York: Free Press, 1958.

——. *A First Language*. Cambridge: Harvard University Press, 1973.

Burge, Tyler. "Demonstrative Constructions, Reference, and Truth." *Journal of Philosophy* 71 (1974) 205–223.

——. "Belief De Re." *Journal of Philosophy* 74 (1977) 338–362.

——. "Individualism and the Mental." *Midwest Studies in Philosophy, IV: Studies in Metaphysics*. Ed. by P. French, T. E. Uehling, and H. Wettstein. Minneapolis: University of Minnesota Press, 1979, 73–121.

——. "Individualism and Psychology." *Philosophical Review* 95 (1986) 284–293.

——. "Wherein is Language Social." *Propositional Attitudes*. Ed. by C. A. Anderson and J. Owens. Stanford, CA: Center for the Study of Language and Information, 1990, 113–130.

Cartwright, Richard. "Identity and Substitutivity." *Identity and Individuation*. Ed. by M. Munitz. New York: New York University Press, 1971, 119–133.

Castañeda, Hector-Neri. "'He': A Study in the Logic of Self-Consciousness." *Ratio* 8 (1966) 130–157.

——. "Indicators and Quasi-Indicators." *American Philosophical Quarterly* 4 (1967) 85–100.

——. "On the Logic of Attributions of Self-Knowledge to Others." *Journal of Philosophy* 65 (1968) 439–456.

——. "Reference, Reality and Perceptual Fields." *Proceedings of the American Philosophical Association* 53 (1980) 763–823.

Chastain, Charles. "Reference and Context." *Minnesota Studies in Philoso-phy of Science.* Vol. 7. Ed. by Keith Gunderson. Minneapolis: University of Minnesota Press, 1975, 194–269.

Chomsky, Noam. *Aspects of the Theory of Syntax.* Cambridge: MIT Press, 1965.

———. *Reflections on Language.* New York: Random, 1975.

Cresswell, M. J. *Logics and Languages.* London: Methuen, 1973.

Cropper, William H. *The Quantum Physicists.* New York: Oxford University Press, 1970.

Cummins, Robert. *The Nature of Psychological Explanation.* Cambridge: MIT Press, 1983.

Currie, Gregory. *Frege, An Introduction to His Philosophy.* Sussex: Harvester, 1982.

Davidson, Donald. "Truth and Meaning." *Synthese* (1967) 304–323. Reprint in *Inquiries into Truth and Interpretation.* Oxford: Clarendon Press, 1984, 17–36.

———. *Inquiries into Truth and Interpretation.* Oxford: Clarendon Press, 1984.

Davidson, Donald, and Harman, Gilbert (eds.). *Semantics of Natural Language.* Dordrecht: Reidel, 1972.

Dennett, Daniel. "Beyond Belief." *Thought and Object.* Edited by A. Woodfield. Oxford: Oxford University Press, 1982.

Devitt, Michael. *Designation.* New York: Columbia University Press, 1981.

———. "Thoughts and Their Ascription." *Midwest Studies in Philosophy* 9 (1984) 385–420.

Donnellan, Keith. "Reference and Definite Descriptions." *Philosophical Review* 75 (1966) 281–304; Reprint in *Naming, Necessity, and Natural Kinds,* ed. by S. Schwartz. Ithaca: Cornell University Press, 1977, 42–65.

———. "Putting Humpty Dumpty Together Again." *Philosophical Review* 77 (1968) 203–215.

———. "Proper Names and Identifying Descriptions." *Synthese* 21 (1970) 335–358.

———. "Speaking of Nothing." *Philosophical Review* 83 (1974) 3–32.

———. "Speaker Reference, Descriptions, and Anaphora." *Syntax and Semantics.* Vol. 9. *Pragmatics,* ed. by P. Cole. New York: Academic Press, 1978, 47–68.

Dowty, David R., Wall, R. E., Peters, S. *Introduction to Montague Semantics*. Dordrecht: Reidel, 1981.

Dretske, Fred I. "Laws of Nature." *Philosophy of Science* 44 (1977) 248–268.

———. *Knowledge and the Flow of Information*. Cambridge: MIT Press, 1981.

Evans, Gareth. *The Varieties of Reference*. Oxford: Oxford University Press, 1982.

———. "Pronouns, Quantifiers and Relative Clauses (I)." *Canadian Journal of Philosophy* 7 (1977); Reprint in *Reference, Truth and Reality*. Ed. by Mark Platts. London: Routledge, 1980, 255–317.

Fillmore, Charles J. "The Case for Case." In *Universals in Linguistic Theory*. Ed. by E. Bach and R. Harms. New York: Holt, Rinehart and Winston, 1968, 1–88.

Fodor, Janet Dean. *Semantics: Theories of Meaning in Generative Grammar*. New York: Crowell, 1977.

———. *The Linguistic Description of Opaque Contexts*. New York: Garland, 1979.

Frege, Gottlob. *Begriffsschrift, eine der arithmetischen nachgebildete Formelsprache des reinen Denkens*. Halle: Nebert, 1879; Reprint in Angelelli, I. (ed.). *Begriffsschrift und andere Aufsaetze*. Hildesheim: Olm, 1964, vii–88.

———. "On Sense and Reference." trans. by M. Black, *Philosophical Writings of Gottlob Frege*. Oxford: Blackwell, 1950, 56–78.

———. "The Thought: A Logical Inquiry." *Mind* 65 (1956), 289–311; Reprint in P. F. Stawson, *Philosophical Logic*. Oxford: Oxford University Press, 1967, 17–38.

Friedman, Michael. "Explanation and Scientific Understanding." *Journal of Philosophy* 71 (1974) 5–14.

Geach, Peter. *Reference and Generality*. Ithaca: Cornell University Press, 1962.

Gibson, James. *The Senses Considered as Perceptual Systems*. Boston: Houghton Mifflin, 1966.

———. *The Ecological Approach to Visual Perception*. Boston: Houghton Mifflin, 1979.

Grice, Paul. "Logic and Conversation." *Syntax and Semantics*. Ed. by P. Cole and J. Morgan 3 (1975) 41–58.

Groenendijk, J., Janssen, T., and Stokhof, M. (eds.). *Truth, Interpretation, and Information*. Dordrecht: Foris, 1984.

Harman, Gilbert. *Thought*. Princeton: Princeton University Press, 1973.

Harré, Rom. *Theories and Things*. London: Sheed and Ward, 1961.

———. *Varieties of Realism*. Oxford: Blackwell, 1987.

Heim, Irene. "File Change Semantics and the Familiarity Theory of Definiteness." *Meaning, Use, and Interpretation of Language*. Ed. by Rainer Baeuerle, Christoph Schwarze, Arnim von Stechow. Berlin: de Gruyter, 1983, 164–189.

Hintikka, Jaakko. "Semantics for Propositional Attitudes." *Philosophical Logic*. Ed. by J. W. Davis et al. Dordrecht: Reidel, 1969, 21–45; Reprint in *Reference and Modality*. Ed. by L. Linsky. Oxford: Oxford University Press, 1971, 145–167.

Hintikka, Jaakko, Moravcsik, J., and Suppes, P. (eds.). *Approaches to Natural Language*. Dordrecht: Reidel, 1973.

Hornsby, Jennifer. "Singular Terms in Context of Propositional Attitude." *Mind* 86 (1977) 31–48.

Houghton, David. *"De Re* Existential Beliefs." *Ratio* 29 (1987) 136–147.

Inwagen, Peter van. "Indexicality and Actuality." *Philosophical Review* 89 (1980) 403–426.

Isard, Stephen. "Changing the Context." *Formal Semantics of Natural Language*. Ed. by E. Keenan. Cambridge: Cambridge University Press, 1975, 287–296.

Jackendoff, Ray S. *Semantic Interpretation in Generative Grammar*. Cambridge: MIT Press, 1972.

Jacobs, P. A. and Rosenbaum, P. S. (eds.). *Readings in English Transformational Grammar*. Waltham: Blaisdell, 1970.

Kamp, Hans. "A Theory of Truth and Semantic Representation." *Truth, Interpretation, and Information*. Ed. by J. Groenendijk, T. Janssen, M. Stokhof. Dordrecht: Foris, 1984, 1–41.

———. "Prolegomena to a Structural Theory of Belief and Other Attitudes." *Propositional Attitudes*. Ed. by C. A. Anderson and J. Owens. Stanford: Center for the Study of Language and Information, 1990, 113–130.

Kaplan, David. "Dthat." *Syntax and Semantics* 9 (1978) 221–243.

———. "Demonstratives." *Themes from Kaplan*. Ed. by Joseph Almog, John Perry, and Howard Wettstein. New York: Oxford, 1989a, 481–563.

———. "Afterthoughts." *Themes from Kaplan*. Ed. by Joseph Almog, John Perry, and Howard Wettstein. New York: Oxford, 1989b, 565–614.

Karttunen, Lauri. "Discourse Referents." *Indiana University Linguistics Club*, 1971, 1–21.

Kearns, John T. *Using Language*. Albany: State University of New York Press, 1984.

Keenan, Edward L. (ed.). *Formal Semantics of Natural Language*. Cambridge: Cambridge University Press, 1975.

Kitcher, Philip. "The Nativist's Dilemma." *Philosophical Quarterly* 28 (1978) 1–16.

Kneale, William. *Probability and Induction*. Oxford: Clarendon Press, 1949.

Kneale, William, and Kneale, Martha. *The Development of Logic*. Oxford: Clarendon Press, 1962.

Krech, David, Crutchfield, R. S., and Livson, N. *Elements of Psychology*. New York: Knopf, 1969.

Kripke, Saul A. "Identity and Necessity." In *Identity and Individuation*. Ed. by M. Munitz and P. Unger. New York: New York University Press, 1971; Reprint in *Naming, Necessity, and Natural Kinds*. Ed. by S. Schwartz. Ithaca: Cornell University Press, 1977, 66–101.

——. "Speaker's Reference and Semantic Reference." *Midwest Studies in Philosophy*. Vol. 2: *Studies in the Philosophy of Language*. Ed. by P. French, T. Uehling, Jr., and H. Wettstein, 1977, 255–276.

——. *Naming and Necessity*. Cambridge: Harvard University Press, 1980.

Kuhn, Thomas. *The Copernican Revolution*. Cambridge: Harvard University Press, 1957.

——. *The Structure of Scientific Revolutions*. Chicago: University of Chicago Press, 1970.

Lakoff, George. *Women, Fire, and Dangerous Things*. Chicago: University of Chicago Press, 1987.

Lewis, David. "Counterpart Theory and Quantified Modal Logic." *Journal of Philosophy* 65 (1968), 113–126.

——. "General Semantics." *Semantics of Natural Language*. Ed. by D. Davidson and G. Harman. Dordrecht: Reidel, 1972, 169–218.

——. *Counterfactuals*. Cambridge: Harvard University Press, 1973.

——. "Scorekeeping in a Language Game." *Journal of Philosophical Logic* 8 (1979) 339–359.

Levinson, Stephen C. *Pragmatics*. London: Cambridge University Press, 1983.

Li, Charles, and Thompson, Sandra. "Subject and Topic, a New Typology of Language." In *Subject and Topic*. Ed. by Charles Li. New York: Academic Press, 1976.

Linsky, Leonard. "Substitutivity." *Journal of Philosophy* 62 (1965) 139–144.

———. (ed.). *Reference and Modality*. Oxford: Oxford University Press, 1971.

———. *Oblique Contexts*. Chicago: University of Chicago Press, 1983.

Locke, John. *An Essay Concerning Human Understanding*. Ed. by A. C. Fraser, 2 vols. New York: Dover, 1959.

Lockwood, Michael. "Identity and Reference." *Identity and Individuation*. Ed. by M. Munitz. New York: New York University Press, 1971, 199–211.

Loux, M. J. (ed.). *The Possible and Actual*. Ithaca, Cornell University Press, 1979.

Lycan, William G. "The Trouble with Possible Worlds." *The Possible and the Actual*. Ed. by M. J. Loux. Ithaca: Cornell University Press, 1979, 274–316.

———. *Logical Form in Natural Language*. Cambridge: MIT Press, 1984.

Lyons, John. "Deixis as the Source of Reference." *Formal Semantics of Natural Language*. Ed. by E. Keenan. Cambridge: Cambridge University Press, 1975, 61–83.

———. *Semantics*. Vols. 1 and 2. London: Cambridge University Press, 1977a, and 1977b (respectively).

McCawley, James D. "Where Do Noun Phrases Come From?" *Readings in English Transformational Grammar*. Ed. by P. A. Jacobs, and P. S. Rosenbaum. Waltham: Blaisdell, 1970, 166–183.

McCawley, James D. "Presupposition and Discourse Structure." *Syntax and Semantics* 11 (1979) 371–388.

McGinn, Colin. "The Mechanism of Reference." *Synthese* 49 (1981) 157–186.

———. "The Structure of Content." *Thought and Object*. Ed. by A. Woodfield. Oxford: Clarendon Press, 1982, 207–258.

MacKay, Alfred F. "Mr. Donnellan and Humpty Dumpty on Referring." *Philosophical Review* 77 (1968) 197–202.

Marcus, Ruth Barcan. "The Identity of Individuals in a Strict Functional Calculus of Second Order." *The Journal of Symbolic Logic* 12 (1947) 12–15.

———. "Modalities and Intensional Languages." *Synthese* 13 (1961) 303–322.

————. "Discussion of the Paper on Ruth Barcan Marcus." *Synthese* 14 (1962) 132–143.

————. "Does the Principle of Substitutivity Rest on a Mistake?" *The Logical Enterprise.* Ed. by A. R. Anderson, R. B. Marcus, and R. M. Martin. New Haven: Yale University Press, 1975, 31–38.

Martinich, A. P. *Communication and Reference.* Berlin: de Gruyter, 1984.

Mates, Benson. "Synonymity." *Meaning and Interpretation.* University of California Publications in Philosophy, 25 (1950) 201–226.

Millikan, Ruth Garrett. *Language, Thought, and other Biological Categories.* Cambridge: MIT Press, 1984.

Morris, Charles W. *Foundations of the Theory of Signs.* Vol. 1, Number 2, *International Encyclopedia of Unified Science.* Chicago: University of Chicago Press, 1938.

Morris, Thomas V. *Understanding Identity Statements.* Aberdeen: Aberdeen University Press, 1984.

Moulton, John, and Roberts, Lawrence D. "An AI Model for Indexical Reference: Input from and Output to Conceptual Graphs." *Proceedings of the Sixth Annual Workshop on Conceptual Graphs.* Binghamton, 1991, 259–268.

————. "A Hybrid Model for Indexical Use in Natural Language." *Journal of Experimental and Theoretical Artificial Intelligence* 4 (1992) 141–148.

Munitz, Milton, and Unger, Peter (eds.). *Identity and Individuation.* New York: New York University Press, 1971.

————. *Semantics and Philosophy.* New York: New York University Press, 1974.

Nagel, Ernest. *Logic Without Metaphysics.* Glencoe: The Free Press, 1956.

Neisser, Ulric. "Visual Search." *Scientific American,* June 1964; Reprint in *Contemporary Psychology.* Ed. by Richard C. Atkinson. San Francisco: Freeman, 1971, 178–185.

Nelson, Raymond. "The Competence-Performance Distinction in Mental Philosophy." *Synthese* 39 (1978) 337–382.

Ogden, C. K., and Richards, I. A. *The Meaning of Meaning.* New York: Harcourt Brace Jovanovich, 1946.

Ochs, Elinor, and Schieffelin, Bambi. *Acquiring Conversational Competence.* London: Routledge, 1983.

Partee, Barbara Hall. "Opacity, Coreference, and Pronouns." *Synthese* 21 (1970) 359–385.

―――. "The Semantics of Belief-Sentences." *Approaches to Natural Language.* Ed. by J. Hintikka. Dordrecht: 1973, 309–336.

―――. "Semantics—Mathematics or Psychology." *Semantics from Different Points of View.* Ed. by R. Baeuerle, U. Egli, and A. von Stechow. Berlin: Springer-Verlag, 1979, 1–14.

―――. "Montague Grammar, Mental Representations, and Reality." *Philosophy and Grammar.* Ed. by S. Kanger and S. Oehman. Dordrecht: Reidel, 1980, 59–78.

―――. "Belief Sentences and the Psychology of Meaning." *Processes, Beliefs, and Questions.* Ed. by S. Peters and E. Saarinen. Dordrecht: Reidel, 1982, 87–106.

Peacocke, Christopher. "Proper Names, Reference, and Rigid Designation." In *Meaning, Reference, and Necessity.* Ed. by Simon Blackburn. Cambridge: Cambridge University Press, 1975, 109–132.

Pears, David. *Ludwig Wittgenstein.* New York: Viking, 1970.

Perry, John. "The Problem of the Essential Indexical." *Nous* 13 (1979) 3–21.

―――. "A Problem about Continued Belief." *Pacific Philosophical Quarterly* 61 (1980) 317–332.

―――. "Cognitive Significance and New Theories of Reference." *Nous* 22 (1988) 1–18.

Peters, Stanley, and Saarinen, Esa (eds.). *Processes, Beliefs, and Questions.* Dordrecht: Reidel, 1982.

Plantinga, Alvin. "The Boethian Compromise." *American Philosophical Quarterly* 15 (1978) 129–138.

Platts, Mark (ed.). *Reference, Truth, and Reality.* London: Routledge, 1980.

Putnam, Hilary. *Reason, Truth and History.* Cambridge: Cambridge University Press, 1981.

Quine, W. V. "Quantifiers and Propositional Attitudes." *Journal of Philosophy* 53 (1956); Reprint in *Reference and Modality.* Ed. by L. Linsky. Oxford: Oxford University Press, 1971, 101–111.

―――. *Word and Object.* Cambridge: MIT Press, 1960.

―――. "Reference and Modality." *From a Logical Point of View.* Cambridge: Harvard University Press, 1961, 139–159.

―――. "Ontological Relativity." *Journal of Philosophy* 65 (1965) 185–212; Reprint in *Ontological Relativity and Other Essays.* New York: Columbia University Press, 1969, 26–68.

―――. "Reply to David Kaplan." *The Philosophy of W. V. Quine.* Ed. by Paul A. Schilpp and Lewis Hahn. LaSalle: Open Court, 1986, 289–294.

Reichenbach, Hans. *Elements of Symbolic Logic.* New York: Macmillan, 1947.

Richards, Whitman. "Is Perception for Real?" Paper presented at the conference "Cognition and Representation" at SUNY Buffalo April 5, 1992.

Roberts, Lawrence D. "Kripke's Version of the Referential-Attributive Distinction." Paper read at the Eastern Division meeting of the American Philosophical Association, 1978.

————. "Russell on the Semantics and Pragmatics of Indexicals." *Philosophia*, 1984a, 111–127.

————. "Ambiguity vs. Generality: Removal of a Logical Confusion." *Canadian Journal of Philosophy* 14 (1984b) 295–313.

————. "Problems About Material and Formal Modes in the Necessity of Identity." *Journal of Philosophy* 82 (1985) 562–572.

————. "The Figure-Ground Model for the Explanation of the Determination of Indexical Reference." *Synthese* 68 (1986a) 441–486.

————. "Reflexive Pronouns: Variables Linked to a Verb in a Propositional Function." Paper read at the meeting of the Linguistics Society of America, New York, 1986b.

————. "Intuitions and Ambiguity Tests." *Canadian Journal of Philosophy* 17 (1987) 189–198.

————. "Quantifier Order, Reflexive Pronouns, and Quasi-indexicals." Technical Report, Dept. of Computer Sciences, SUNY Buffalo, 1988.

————. "Three Arguments against Non-semantic Accounts of the Informativeness of Identity Statements." (Ms.) 1992a.

————. "Assertion, Pragmatics, and the Informativeness of Identity Statements." (Ms.) 1992b.

————. "Pure Indexicals vs. True Demonstratives: A Difference in Compactness." (Ms.) 1992c.

————. "The Foundations of Kaplan's Direct Reference Theory." *Philosophia* 23 (1993).

————. "Perry on Indexical Semantics and Belief States." *Communication and Cognition*, forthcoming.

Roberts, Lawrence D.; see also Moulton, John, and Roberts, Lawrence D.

Romanos, George D. *Quine and Analytic Philosophy.* Cambridge: MIT Press, 1983.

Ross, J. R. *Constraints on Variables in Syntax*, Ph.D. diss. Cambridge: MIT, 1967.

Russell, Bertrand. "On Denoting." *Mind*, 1905; Reprint in *Logic and Knowledge*. Ed. by R. C. Marsh. London: Allen, 1956, 41–56.

———. *The Problems of Philosophy*. London: Oxford University Press, 1912.

———. "On the Nature of Acquaintance." Reprint in *Logic and Knowledge*. Ed. by R. C. Marsh. London: Allen, 1914, 1956, 127–174.

———. "The Philosophy of Logical Atomism." Reprint in *Logic and Knowledge*. Ed. by R. C. Marsh. London: Allen, 1918, 1956, 177–281.

Ryle, Gilbert. *The Concept of Mind*. Harmondsworth: Penguin, 1949, 1963.

———. *Dilemmas*. Cambridge: Cambridge University Press, 1954.

———. "The Theory of Meaning." *British Philosophy in Mid-Century*. Ed. by C. A. Mace. London: George Allen and Unwin, 1957.

Saarinen, Esa. "How to Frege a Russell-Kaplan." *Nous* 16 (1982) 253–276.

Salmon, Nathan U. *Reference and Essence*. Princeton: Princeton University Press, 1981.

Schwartz, Stephen P. (ed.). *Naming, Necessity, and Natural Kinds*. Ithaca: Cornell University Press, 1977.

Searle, John. "Proper Names." *Mind* 67 (1958) 166–173.

———. *Speech Acts*. New York: Cambridge University Press, 1969.

———. *Expression and Meaning*. Cambridge: Cambridge University Press, 1979.

———. "Referential and Attributive." *Monist* 62 (1979); Reprint in John Searle, *Expression and Meaning*. Cambridge: Cambridge University Press, 1979, 137–161.

Shapiro, Stuart C., and Rapaport, William J. "SNePS Considered as a Fully Intensional Propositional Semantic Network." *The Knowledge Frontier*. Ed. by N. Cercone and G. McCalla, New York: Springer, 1987, 263–315.

Smith, David Woodruff. "What is the Meaning of 'This'?" *Nous* 16 (1982) 181–208.

Sowa, John. *Conceptual Structures*. Reading: Addison-Wesley, 1984.

Stalnaker, Robert C. "Pragmatics." *The Semantics of Natural Language*. Ed. by D. Davidson and G. Harman. Dordrecht: Reidel, 1972, 380–397.

———. "The Autonomy of Semantics." Paper read at SUNY Binghamton, Nov. 11, 1987.

Stampe, Dennis W. "Attributives and Interrogatives." *Semantics and Philosophy.* Ed. by M. K. Munitz and P. K. Unger. New York: New York University Press, 1974, 159–196.

Stich, Stephen. *From Folk Psychology to Cognitive Science.* Cambridge: MIT Press, 1983.

Strawson, Peter F. "On Referring." *Mind* 59 (1950) 320–344; Reprint in *Philosophy and Ordinary Language.* Ed. by Charles E. Caton. Urbana: University of Illinois Press, 1963, 162–193.

———. *Individuals.* London: Methuen, 1959; Reprint New York: Doubleday, 1963.

———. "Singular Terms and Predication." *Journal of Philosophy* 58 (1961) 393–412.

———. "Identifying Reference and Truth Values." *Theoria* 30 (1964) 96–118.

———. *Subject and Predicate in Logic and Grammar.* London: Methuen, 1974.

Swoyer, Chris. "Belief and Predication." *Nous* 17 (1984) 197–220.

Taylor, Barry. "Truth-Theory for Indexical Languages." *Reference, Truth, and Reality.* Ed. by Mark Platts. London: Routledge, 1980, 182–198.

Urmson, J. O. "Criteria of Intensionality." *Proceedings of the Aristotelian Society.* Vol. 42, suppl. (1968) 107–122.

Walker, Jearl. "The Amateur Scientist." *Scientific American* 238 (1978) 154–162.

Weinstein, Scott. "Truth and Demonstratives." *Nous* 8 (1974) 179–184.

Wettstein, Howard K. "Indexical Reference and Propositional Content." *Philosophical Studies* 36 (1979) 91–100.

———. "How to Bridge the Gap Between Meaning and Reference." *Synthese* 58 (1984) 63–84.

———. "Has Semantics Rested on a Mistake?" *Journal of Philosophy* 83 (1986) 185–209.

———. "Cognitive Significance without Cognitive Content." *Themes from Kaplan.* Ed. by Joseph Almog, John Perry, and Howard Wettstein. New York: Oxford, 1989, 421–454.

———. "Response to John Perry's 'Cognitive Significance and New Theories of Reference.'" Ms. April 24, 1988.

Wilson, George. "On Definite and Indefinite Descriptions." *Philosophical Review* 87 (1978) 48–76.

Winograd, Terry. "Moving the Semantic Fulcrum." *Linguistics and Philosophy* 8 (1984) 91–104.

Wittgenstein, Ludwig. *Philosophical Investigations*. Oxford: Blackwell, 1953.

Woodfield, A. (ed.). *Thought and Object*. Oxford: Oxford University Press, 1982.

Name Index

Achinstein, P., 136–137, 167
Alston, W., 2
Aristarchus, 6
Aristotle, 20, 101, 154, 166
Aronson, J., 4, 170
Atlas, J., 150, 159

Bach, K., 87, 150, 151, 155, 158, 162, 164
Bar-Hillel, Y., 8
Barwise, J., 151
Bell, J., 163
Berger, A., 145
Beskin, J., 157
Bohr, N., 6
Born, M., 152
Brinton, A., 153, 156, 162
Brown, R., 2, 17
Burge, T., 12, 146, 151, 153, 162

Cartwright, R., 168
Castaneda, H., 154, 169
Chomsky, N., 1, 12, 153
Cresswell, M., 151
Cropper, W., 150, 152
Crutchfield, R., 154
Cummins, R., 149
Currie, G., 167

Davidson, D., 150
Dennett, D., 168
Devitt, M., 145, 162
Donnellan, K., 7, ch. 4, 145, 156, 160, 162, 165
Dowty, D., 150
Dretske, F., 4, 137

Evans, G., 45, 135, 136, 152, 153, 158, 161, 165

Fillmore, C., 9
Fodor, J., 166, 167
Frege, G., 4, 16, 18, 98, 105, 106, 109, 112, 166, 167
Friedman, 149

Geach, P., 75, 116, 163, 170
Gibson, J., 49, 159
Grice, P., 150, 160
Gross, P., 157

Harman, G., 13
Harre, R., 4, 152, 159
Harris, R., 152
Heim, I., 163
Hempel, C., 168
Hicetas, 6
Hornsby, J., 70
Houghton, D., 139

Inwagen, P. van, 156
Isard, S., 164

Jackendoff, R., 165

Kamp, H., 151, 163
Kaplan, D., 38, 51–52, 151, 153, 154, 156, 160, 162
Karttunen, L., 87
Kearns, J., 109, 167
Kepler, J., 5
Kitcher, P., 153
Kneale, M., 167

187

Subject Index

Ambiguity, 69–70, 135, 140, 161
Activity vs. achievement, 101, 166
Affordances, 159
Analyses vs. mechanisms, 11–12, 61, 111–12
Anaphora, 159, 161. *See also* Ground, discourse-dependent context
Anaphora, E-type, 45, 135–36, 140
Aprioricity, 8–10, 12, 25, 107, 113, 114, 117, 151, 152
Artificial intelligence, 9, 150, 155
Assertion, 68, 69
Atom, 6
Attention directing, 17, 22, 99, 155–56, 158
Attention directing model for reference, 96–105, 107–11, 114–15, 117, 119–20, 122, 126, 132–35, 141, 143, 146, 147, 163, 169
  identificatory (for audience) function, 96–100, 110, 114, 117–18, 143–46
  relating function, 96–100, 110, 112, 114–16, 118, 119, 127, 140–41, 143, 165, 166
  specificatory function, 96–100, 108–12, 116–32, 135, 137, 140, 141, 143, 144, 146, 165, 166, 167, 169, 170
Attribute identity contexts, 129–30, 141, 169

Background. *See* Figure-ground model, ground
Belief contexts. *See* Propositional attitudes

Bottom-up vs. top-down theorizing, 7, 9, 10, 38, 51–52, 107

Calculus, 152
Cancelling out fallacy, 116
Case, 99–100
Causal-chain theories, 145–46, 154
Cause-effect relations, 42–43, 137
Character, 51
Chemical analysis vs. mechanisms, 11–12
Circular devices, 5, 166
Cognitive content, 9, 146–47
Communication, 102, 151; arguments based on, 25–31, 62–63
Communicational paradigm, 11–14
Comparison and opacity, 139, 141
Compositionality, 1, 7
Content, 51
Context, 15, 20, 22, 41–51, 169; contributes to figure, 22, 24; need for more than one sentence, 75; psychological bases for containment in, 49–50. *See also* Figure-ground model, ground
Conventions, 73, 102
Coordinate systems, 28
Coreferentiality. *See* Figure-ground model, ground, discourse-dependent context

|De dicto| vs. |de re|, 127–29
Definite descriptions: attributive and referential uses of, 55–73, 144, 155, 156, 158, 160–64, 169; compared to the specific vs. non-specific distinc-

189